STEM MOMS

STEM MMS

Design, Build, and Test
to Create the Work-Life of Your Dreams

✧

CASSIE LEONARD

2023 Edition

ELMM PRESS
SEATTLE

Published by ELMM Press
Seattle, Washington
www.elmm.press

Note: The strategies and advice in this book are based upon the research and the personal and professional experiences of the author. The publisher makes no guarantees concerning the level of success you may experience by following the strategies contained herein, and you accept the risk that results will differ for each reader. If you have any questions or concerns about the information in this book, please consult with a qualified professional.

Credits:
Cover design by Romana Bovan
Cover Element: *Texture, Background Smooth* by BarbaraALane via Pixabay. This image is licensed under the Pixabay Free Commercial License.
Paper Airplane Doodle Element by Papermax Studio via Canva.com. This graphic is licensed under the Canva Free Media License Agreement
Custom artwork was created by Moon S (@ingeniousarts) via Fiverr.
All additional graphics are from Canva's Content Library. These graphics are licensed under the Canva Content License Agreement.
Margaret Bonanno, *A Certain Slant of Light*. New York. Seaview Books: trade distribution by Simon & Schuster. Copyright © 1979, 2017 by Margaret Wander Bonanno. Reprinted with permission.

Paperback Edition

ISBN 979-8-9887205-0-8 (paperback)
ISBN 979-8-9887205-1-5 (ebook)

Printed in the United States of America
First Edition

To Aunt Anne, for being an engineer, leader, and mom, and inspiring me to do the same long before I had any idea it wasn't the norm.

To all my wonderful mentors who have donated their precious time to support me. You are so appreciated.

CONTENTS

CHAPTER 5

CONCLUSION

INTRODUCTION

FOR STEM MOMS+

I am Cassie.

I am an engineer, leader, and mother. And because I'm an engineer, I decided there really should be an acronym for this… ELM.

During the 26 years since first choosing STEM (science, technology, engineering, and mathematics), I have regularly felt completely unique—being the only woman in a class or meeting is unfortunately the norm.

When I chose to have children and pursue management, I unintentionally set myself apart yet again. As a STEM mom in growing leadership roles, I found I was quickly running short on role models. As you might have experienced yourself, this was very disheartening.

The first time I worked for a senior leader who was also a mother was an eye-opening experience. I realized how isolated I had felt up until that point, even though I had never taken the time to ponder it. I had assumed it was just the way it was.

In 2021 this new boss of mine and I were invited to participate on a panel at the Society of Women Engineers (SWE) National Conference in Indianapolis. We shared the stage with three more fantastic moms with highly technical leadership roles. The panel was called "Shared Experience as Women Leaders and Working Moms." Despite overhearing a few snickers in the hall and even one young woman quipping, "who would even go to that," the room was packed. I was both thrilled and nervous.

Thankfully, it turned out to be an hour of engaging questions, conversations, laughter, and highly personal sharing. It reminded me (or maybe taught me for the first time) how many women out there have similar hopes and goals. It also made me wonder how many of us might occasionally feel like we are on a one-woman island, forging our own path blindly.

I have written *STEM Moms* to empower women, mothers, engineers, STEM goddesses—whatever title you resonate with. This book is offered as a tool to help you find your footing and to do it in such a way that you flourish!

I present this through the lens of a woman who has built a career in a male-dominated technical field, but I hope many take-aways are transferable to any situation.

I offer the tools and methods in this book humbly. I am not a scholar, and up until now I didn't consider myself a writer either. I am however a woman who has personally found that STEM leadership and living a fun and fulfilling life at the same time is a future worth pursuing.

A bit more about me, following the now well-established ELM acronym:

Engineer: I earned a bachelor's in aerospace engineering from UCLA and a master's in aerodynamics from the University of Sheffield in England. I started at Boeing in 2006, structurally analyzing commercial derivative aircraft. The coolest title I held was P-8 Delivery Captain—I wish that one came with a hat.

Leader: Eight years into my career, I opted for management. I stepped into formal leadership with a team of 33 engineers. From there I progressed to senior roles, leading across programs, customers, contracts, and coasts. My focus is always the people, as I wholeheartedly believe the best products come from engaged teams.

Mom: I am a mother of two wonderful boys. I have an awesome husband, my partner in life, who is crushing a technical leadership career of his own. We have a very loving supportive family scattered across the country and globe (great for vacation destinations, not useful at all for date nights).

When Seattle Public Schools shut down in March 2020, we adjusted. I spent 18 months with two kids staring at me while I tried to work. I led design reviews while secretly listening to hear if my kindergartener was staying focused on Zoom. I learned tools and tricks to maintain sanity and cope with the inevitable guilt. I dug deep into my bag of skills to manage day to day and keep focused on what really matters.

Now that schools are back, I have time to share that learning with you!

And a secret fourth trait I encourage everyone to build:

Mentor: (Queue the new acronym: ELMM!) I was lucky enough to be paired with a highly successful engineer-leader-mom-mentor when I was just starting out. She guided me from new-hire to my first management role. I started mentoring others as soon as anyone seemed to care what I had to share, which was surprisingly early in my career.

Today, having "retired" from corporate aerospace, I am a full-time mentor. As founder of ELMM Coaching, I work with STEM moms to help them grow fearlessly and to connect whole-heartedly. Much of what I offer in coaching and within this book is rooted in lessons I learned from my own mentors. I listened closely, asked questions, and put each concept to the test. While many tools have grown and changed from the first mentoring meetings, the original concepts are still intact.

Creating Our Space

Congratulations on being amazing already!

If you picked up this book, it is likely you are excited by technical challenges. You might have a family, or maybe you don't. Maybe you are curious about the idea of potentially maybe sort of someday having a variation of a family. All are valid and welcome in this space.

On top of STEM skills and an interest in caregiving, I'll wager you also have, or want to develop, leadership skills. As industries change and grow, leadership is becoming an essential skill set for everyone, not just those at the very top.

By investing now in communication, organization, sincerity, passion, and trust (to name a few), you will lay a foundation for your ability to create your best life.

Did you know:

Over 3 million women and LGBTQIA+ individuals work in STEM fields today.

If you are pursuing a life that incorporates parenthood, leadership, and technical challenge, *and* you don't identify male, you are part of a very special community. One friend whimsically referred to three of us at an ad hoc technical women's happy hour as "a herd of unicorns."

Currently more than 3 million US-based women and LGBTQIA+ people work in STEM fields.[1] I hope that by sharing my story, and supporting you in yours, we can build momentum to grow our community.

This book is intended to be a beacon for anyone seeking solutions to live their best life. We will celebrate our skills and achievements, and with personal stories and activities throughout, you will quickly discover you are not alone!

Who is this Book for?

Short Answer: You!

---

[1] 3,083,097 to be inaccurately precise. Unfortunately, there is almost no data on how many LGBTQIA+ people in the United States work in STEM. We do know from an Imperial Medical Blog study is that LGBT people are under-represented by roughly 20%. As the representative study's title suggests, "STEM needs to face up to its problem with LGBT diversity." blogs.imperial.ac.uk. 2019.
See Chapter 5, "Being Us" for expanded details on this calculation.

Longer Answer:

Moms and caregivers who are searching for balance. This includes, but is not limited to, people just starting to plan for a family and those who want to spend more time with the loved ones they have. Parenthood has many different and beautiful expressions. I use the term *Mom* because this is my lens (actually, my children call me Momma). If you don't resonate with this word choice, please know you are still welcome.

If you are earlier on your journey, you might not know if you want any of this. Don't worry, the tools and stories coming up are shared as only one perspective. Consider them as you see fit.

Allies: You're welcome too! Do you want to gain understanding of the challenges others at your workplace face? You might be the partner of someone who is charting a course in STEM. While much of this book's narrative will not specifically be directed to you, I am thankful you are here and committed to learning.

Watch for this ally badge throughout the book for thoughts, ideas, and relatively simple actions you can take today to make a difference.

Still not sure?

Here is a quick quiz for you. Hopefully it reminds you of a magazine quiz from your youth, or maybe your team's more recent awkward but slightly fun ice breaker.

Pop Quiz
THIS OR THAT ICEBREAKER

In each row, select an option that resonates with you.
Don't think too hard, and have fun!

This	That	Both	Neither
Spreadsheets	Crayons	Both	Neither
Calculators	Power drills	Both	Neither
Being a caregiver	Being a leader	Both	Neither
Delivering an awesome presentation	Reading a bedtime story with all the voices	Both	Neither
Being healthy	Being happy	Both	Neither
Financial independence	Going on bold new adventures	Both	Neither
Rocking a career	Living my best life	Both	Neither
Being a mentor	Learning every day	Both	Neither
Being present for others	Making time for self-care	Both	Neither

continue to scoring >>

Scoring

Count the number of times you circled answers in each column.
Write that number on the lines below.

Count of *This* _____

Count of *That* _____

Count of *Both* _____

Count of *Neither* _____

Results

If ((This + That) > 0) ⟶ You have clarity on what you love in life. This book will translate your goals and values into amazing actions and strategies.

If (Both > 0) ⟶ This book is made for you. You are walking the line between seeming opposites. Together, we'll uncover how your many passions and skills can be assets that help you excel towards your goals!

If (Neither > 0) ⟶ Nice. This is just a reminder you have agency on this journey.

If (Neither > 8) ⟶ This book may not be a perfect fit for your journey, but it could be a great way to glimpse another's. The choice is yours!

Ally

Why Does It Matter?

STEM Moms is a tool for you to start using today. It is also a call to action—let's build up others as we go.

We can eliminate the loneliness women and caregivers in technical careers experience on their own secret islands. We can reach out to others and build a shared identity.

We have unique skills and experiences. We get to live the joys and trials of parenting. We get to solve the stickiest technical problems for this world of ours. We do all this in valiant opposition to societal norms that continuously forget to celebrate that we can.

We live in a world where girls continue to hear what they *should* do, or what they are more likely to be *good* at. It is a systemic bias rooted in our history, but unfortunately still abundant today. This often-unconscious bias manifests in many forms starting at very young ages.

For example:

- Parents statistically spend more time reading and storytelling with their daughters, while boys are exposed to more spatial language in their earliest years.[2]
- Teachers tend to perceive girls as on par with boys in math only if they also demonstrate they are working harder than the boys.[3]
- Girls', but not boys', exposure to STEM activities is contingent on expressed intertest.[4]

---

[2] See Sean F Reardon, Erin M Fahle, Demetra Kalogrides, Anne Podolsky, and Rosalia C Zarate. "Gender achievement gaps in U.S. school districts." Stanford CEPA. June 2018.

[3] See Joseph R Cimpian, Sarah T Lubienski, Martha B Makowski, and Emily K Miller. "Have gender gaps in math closed? Achievement, teacher perceptions, and learning behaviors across two ECLS-K cohorts." Sage Journals. 2016.

[4] See Joyce M Alexander, Kathy E Johnson, and Ken Kelley. "Longitudinal analysis of the relations between opportunities to learn about science and the development of interests related to science." Wiley Online Library. June 28, 2012.

Media continues this propagation of occupational segregation and stereotypes through who is shown on screen. 62.9% of TV and movie characters in STEM careers are male.[5]

Strong female STEM characters matter. Dana Scully caught people's attention when she showed up as a primetime multi-dimensional woman in STEM back in 1993. The *Scully effect* has significantly changed the face of science and engineering. This one dynamic character (played exquisitely by Gillian Anderson) increased female viewers interest in STEM by 50%. Moreover, 63% of women in STEM today cite Scully as a role model.[6]

Fortunately, the numbers are trending up, but we still have a ways to go. The lasting effects of only the most resilient girls making it into *boy jobs* over the past century means we have fewer role models today to look to for guidance.

Those of us who persevere through college, start a technical career where we can apply our unique and diverse skills, and stick with it through promotions and leadership roles, have an opportunity and responsibility to shout from the rooftops—women belong in STEM!

By sharing our experiences out loud, we can encourage more girls, women, LGBTQIA+ people, and really stellar mommas to join us.

What's in Store for You?

First and foremost, remember… you are not alone, and it can be done.

When I was growing up in the 1980s, I was blessed with naivety and some truly amazing ELM role models. I heard consistently that women could do anything they wanted. With an aunt running her own civil engineering firm, and my dad's mechanical engineering boss stopping by

---

[5] See The Lyda Hill Foundation & The Geena Davis Institute on Gender in Media. "Portray Her: Representations of women STEM characters in media." SeeJane.org. 2023.
[6] See Geena Davis Institute on Gender in Media. "The Scully Effect: I want to believe in STEM." SeeJane.org. 2023.

with her daughter for playdates, I thought it was perfectly normal to want to be an engineer myself.

And since I was told I could do ANYTHING, I decided it would be great to be very successful, have a family, and be a boss too. Why not?!

I was so ready to do it all that in my sixth-grade yearbook I am quoted saying, "when I grow up, I want to make more money than my husband." I was a hero to all the moms at school. There was one problem though. I never considered at the wise old age of 11, or for many years after, that salary might not be the only way to measure my best life.

These days I spend time pondering these questions:

- Is it possible we don't need all of everything all the time?
- What if we had clarity on what was most important to us and the people we care most about?
- Would we feel more comfortable in our own choices?
- Would we be empowered to say "no" to unnecessary stressors?
- Could we feel less guilt through it all?

It might be possible...

We are going on an adventure together. We'll have activities and time to think and reflect along the way as we strategize for professional and personal success, satisfaction, and balance!

Throughout this book, we're going to investigate skills that are unique only to you. We'll look at how to leverage each one so you can navigate toward your best life.

In Chapter 1 we'll dig into your transferrable skills—those unique superpowers you have been developing as a parent, leader, and in your

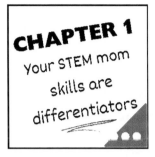

CHAPTER 1
Your STEM mom skills are differentiators

career of choice. We'll assess how this toolbox of always available resources sets you apart from the crowd.

Activities:

- Transferable Skills Pre-Work
- Transferable Skills Venn Diagram
- Reflection Space: Transferable Skills

CHAPTER 2
set big goals aligned to your values

In Chapter 2 we'll look at what's truly important to you. We'll review tools to help you shape your personal and professional goals, and then we'll build synergy between the two.

Activities:

- Aspirations Deep Dive
- Reflection Space: Goals & Values
- YOLO Chalkboard Group Activity
- Top 10 Pre-Work, Six Ws
- My Top 10 List

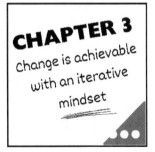

CHAPTER 3
change is achievable with an iterative mindset

In Chapter 3 we'll embrace the iterative design process to investigate your assumptions and begin making micro-adjustments toward the goals you most want to achieve.

Activities:

- Audacious, Career, and Fulfilling Life Markers, 5 Year Map Pre-Work
- 5 Year Maps
- Somatic Markers Checkpoint

CHAPTER 4

Any transition is manageable with a few checklists

In Chapter 4 we'll learn tools to successfully navigate life's larger transitions with some emotional resilience. A thoughtful strategy will help you deliver results quicker and possibly enjoy the ride more. Here we'll tackle how to manage the internal struggle and maybe give ourselves a bit of a break too.

Activities:

- Reflection Space: Past Transitions
- Transition Checklists
- Acknowledge Your Saboteur Art Project
- Reflection Space: Taking Your Saboteur's Power
- Prioritization Worksheet

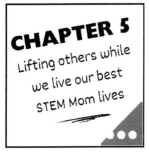

CHAPTER 5

Lifting others while we live our best STEM Mom lives

In Chapter 5 we'll shift gears away from personal discovery and development—it's time to look around.

Who in your world is watching you? Who could you help with a little more attention—be it a formal mentoring partnership or simply a kind word? We might have grown up on female engineer islands, but that doesn't mean the next generation has to. We'll address what you might want to share, and potential avenues through which to do it.

Activities:

- Reflection Space: Sharing Your Journey
- Reflection Space: Designing Your Own Best Life

And then we wrap it all up!

It will be fun and never too heavy, promise. Take your time, reflect, and enjoy. Consider progressing through the book in order, as activities do call back on each other. But if you're super excited to jump to something, go for it. You do you.

Tools you may like to have with you:

- A pen, pencil, or box of markers, depending on your style.
- Coffee, tea, or a cocktail—whatever makes you feel cozy, curious, and creative.
- An open mind.

If you would prefer not to write in a shiny new book, you can find free printable copies of each worksheet at www.elmmcoaching.com. Better yet, write all over this copy to hold as a memento, and get a second copy to lend to your mentees!

If you have any questions, my contact information is also on the website. If you're just so excited to get started and want to tell someone, go ahead and tell the world with #STEMMomsBook.

www.elmmcoaching.com

CHAPTER 1

EMBRACE YOUR SKILLS

Great news—you already have so many skills!

Wherever you are in your *ELMtastic* (new adjective?) journey, you already bring so much to the table. Trust me on this one, I have had some pretty intense opportunities to test out my trifecta of technical, leadership, and life skills in action.

When 2020 dawned, I felt like I was rocking my professional career. I had just finished leading the design review for the most complicated aircraft modification program of this decade, and it was terrific!

At home, my littlest little was in kindergarten—I had survived the years of slogging one kid in school and another to daycare across town. It was time to celebrate and have some well-earned daily me time.

Then... March 11th, 2020, struck. My boys, along with the rest of the Seattle Public School system, were sent home.[1] They said it would be two weeks, but I was pretty sure that's not how pandemics work.

---

[1] The Seattle Public School system was the first major school district in the United States to shut down in the pandemic. While most schools followed suit in the days and weeks to come, those first few days were a whole new isolated island to navigate.

I had a choice:

A) Curl up in a ball and cry, or
B) Figure out what to do with these awesome little humans who still needed to learn, be engaged, and feel like they had some stability in their suddenly entirely isolated lives.

I chose B. (Mostly.)

Risk. Fail. Risk Again.

National Theater Institute
national theaterinstitute.org

The surprising thing was, despite never being a schoolteacher and having rarely spent 16 straight hours in a day with my own children, it did not take long for me to realize I had an arsenal of skills to throw at this new challenge.

Like you, I am a problem solver. At this point I had also managed a whole lot of projects, so why not try to project manage this too?!

First things first, I took the next day off work. There are certain days when you just don't need to be at work. Then, planning.

A basic project management plan includes:

- A clearly defined problem statement.
- Analysis of the constraints.
- A strategy.
- An action plan (ideally complete with names and dates).

Our rapidly prototyped family quarantine plan was not ideal, but it was a starting point:

Problem: The kids need to be safe and engaged, and ideally learning a bit from 7:30 to 4:30 weekdays without any external help.

Constraints: Mom and Dad both have full-time jobs, which we are now trying to do from home as well.

Strategy:

- Set clear expectations for the family.
- Make (or buy) activities that require limited adult support.
- Remind ourselves constantly that we're all in this together; we know this is hard.

Action Plan:

TASK	WHO	WHEN
Make an activities ideas list	Everyone	Now
Co-create expectations	Everyone	Now
Pick a research project	Kids	Soon
Engage grandparents to help via skype	Dad	Soon
Buy workbooks, a printer & craft stuff	Mom	Now
Take kids to the park	Dad	Daily
Help the kids cook something	Mom or Dad	Daily
Block out key chunks on work calendar	Mom & Dad	Soon

I'd love to say it was a beautifully typed spreadsheet at that time, but honestly half of this was in my head, and the other half was a lot of markers, crayons, and deer in headlights looks from all of us.

Throughout the weeks, which turned to months, and ultimately 1.5 years of home schooling, I found flexibility and creativity were critical. Thankfully I've had many other opportunities to develop and practice these skills throughout life and my engineering career.

When new constraints arose, like the closing of all the libraries, we adjusted. Suddenly a gently used paperwhite kindle and a subscription to Libby became our lifeline.

When the kids got super-duper bored, we built up our community. My wonderfully supportive in-laws 8 time zones east of us committed to weekly 2-hour "gra'ma school" video calls to add some variety.

It did not all go well. Some days were terrible, but others were amazing. I am thankful all four of us stayed healthy, and we all still like talking to each other most days. I am also so glad I had a toolbox of skills to get through each day.

As a parent, I leveraged compassion, empathy, and knowing when to not put up with any more crap. More and more, I find I use all these skills at work when I lead and manage others.

As an engineer, I applied my analytical skills. I assessed the risk of the situation quickly (kids are safe and healthy, boredom will be our biggest challenge) and used my love of numbers and science to create new activities for the kids (here's to a day of building mechanized catapults!).

I also picked up a new skill—I can mute and cover my face with my coffee cup before yelling, "Get outside right now!"

I call that a win.

Embedded in any STEM mom and ELM are dozens, or maybe hundreds, of transferable skills. They are our secret to successful technical careers, and they are the key to solving for balance with the rest of our life's aspirations.

Design, Build, Test, Repeat.

Iterate Around Your Technical Skills

I learned it in college. Kids today are learning it in elementary school—design, build, test, repeat.

Such a simple concept, and yet so powerful. It's the foundation of all engineering—think something up, make it, see if it works, and then adjust and repeat from there. It's a beautiful iterative learning process that can be applied broadly. As a STEM professional, when you get stuck, you probably come back to these three simple words too.

So, what does design, build, test have to do with leveraging transferable skills and building a balanced and successful career?

Design, build, test is the foundation of it all!

What you learned, or are learning, in your technical degree is a skill that can be taken outside the lab and applied to everything you do.

It's a mindset. Stay in learning mode, always be willing to iterate, and be comfortable with knowing your first solution is a prototype. It might be a great prototype, but there is more learning to come.

When the schools shut down, we made an action plan, but then things changed, and we adjusted.

I learned a lot in college, but the design, build, test cycle might just be the most important tool I've carried forward with me. Hold this one close as we look at the skills you have learned through your life and career experiences.

Grab a pen. It's time to brainstorm.

As a STEM student or professional, you are on a growth trajectory. Through all your education and career experience you've been collecting technical skills. Whether you are currently studying high school geometry or applying your PhD in multiverse physics, you are a problem solver who can synthesize large amounts of complex data and creatively apply design, build, and test in all that you do.

Take a few minutes to capture all your technical skills you have worked so hard to develop on the next page. On this first of three worksheets, focus just on your technical skills.

Really want to get into it? Before you start this activity, change your clothes to match the role, and put on some music that you would listen to in a technical environment. I'll even help you with suggestions…

Wardrobe: That free branded polo shirt you've never found the right time to wear before.

Music: "Higher Ground" by Odesza.

Transferable Skills Pre-Work
TECHNICAL SKILLS

List your technical skills here. No right or wrong answers, just free flow ideas. We'll consolidate later.

Examples: *Coding, problem solving, solving partial differential equations, woodworking, iteratively designing, marketing, 3D modelling/CAD...*

Show Up as a Leader

A leader is someone people follow. Leadership does not require a formal title or corner office.

I have seen entry-level engineers who are high impact leaders. People who join the team with so much enthusiasm and curiosity—they ask questions, then dive in and do a great job. Their energy is contagious.

I have seen managers who are leaders, and some who are not. Checking on attendance and tasking, attending meetings, and signing timecards is managing. That is not enough to make someone a leader.

The person who actively listens to their team members, seeks out diversity of thought, and incorporates the best of what they learn into thoughtfully communicating their vision is a leader. They remove barriers and support their team when things get tough. People follow them because they trust them.

In my pursuit of being a leader, I have focused on building my communication skills: speaking clearly, listening attentively, under-standing how each person receives feedback best (written, spoken one-on-one, emailed 18 times in bold font...)

I have found that being authentically me resonates with people. I don't try to hide the fact that I have family commitments. I don't hide my sarcasm (although I do note who doesn't appreciate it, and I try to respect that). I dress nicely, but my hair is almost always in a ponytail because that's who I am.

And I show up fully. I sit at the table, and I sit tall. I am here because I bring value to this effort. I am at this meeting because I have things to contribute. Confidence is inspiring. Enthusiasm and energy are contagious. Add a bit of polish in the communication (listening as well as speaking), and you have a strong suite of leadership skills.

Ready for round two of brainstorming? This time... leadership skills.

Wardrobe: Your power suit.

Music: "Unstoppable" by Sia.

Transferable Skills Pre-Work
LEADERSHIP SKILLS

List your leadership skills. Consider all your leadership roles, including work, volunteer, service, school, etc.

Examples: *Presenting, mentoring, defining strategy, setting clear expectations, listening, supporting others, being adaptable, managing risk...*

Rock Your Mom Skills

Possibly the most underrated suite of skills—mom skills.[2] Like Mary Poppins, you carry a seemingly limitless magical bag of tricks with you.

The modern-day working parent has so much on their plate. You are already rocking time management skills, massive systematic coordination skills, and (if you've ever had to fill out back to school forms) an inordinate amount of patience, even when it doesn't feel like you can balance it all.

You are also a daily example of servant leadership—how much of what you do is with someone else's best interest at heart?

Your communication style is authentic. It ranges from very warm (*Sweet dreams, darling*) to highly directive (*Get your shoes on!*) depending on the situation. You have developed the ability to speak very candidly (*That is too much milk*) and to provide immediate recognition (*Look at your drawing! Is it a butterfly?*).

When the going gets tough, you show empathy. You know instinctively when *jump up, you're fine* is appropriate and when to grab the Band-Aids.

Every day is another opportunity to practice setting boundaries.

30 minutes of screen time is plenty…

Don't go out the front door without a parent…

You need to hold my hand to cross the street…

As a parent, you're also developing your ability to function as part of a leadership team. Whether you are flying solo or have a partner, there are many others who you need to collaborate with on a near daily basis: teachers, daycare directors, coaches, maybe your own parents and your in-laws, the next-door neighbor, your best friend—it's a village (whether you want it to be or not).

---

[2] Please mentally remove and replace "mom skills" with whatever term resonates for you. This could be caregiver skills, life skills, awesome auntie skills, or any other skills you're proud of related to living your non-professional life.

Crafting your skills to clearly define expectations and priorities, establish role clarity, and articulate who has ultimate authority for any decisions—these are all crucial skills for at-home success AND are skills that can be transferred to the workplace.

And the list goes on. Just think about your morning routine—multiple wake up calls, reminders to get dressed, brush teeth, find socks, eat breakfasts, then drop off schedules, checking who forgot they have a form you need to sign.

It's sunny, why do I need a jacket?

Can I have a playdate this afternoon?

—project management skills galore!

While often not glamorous, and regularly involving tissues and glitter glue, the adventures of being a working parent have and will continue to transform you into a stronger, more capable person with many tried and tested skills to be shared with the world.

It's time for the third and final round of brainstorming before we transition to consolidating all this work you're doing. Use the next page to list your version of mom skills.

Wardrobe: Whatever you change into at the end of the workday.

Music: "Juice" by Lizzo.[3]

---

[3] Please be advised Lizzo's masterpiece of a song is explicit. If that is not your style, try "Halo" by Beyonce and imagine she's singing directly to you.

Transferable Skills Pre-Work
MOM / LIFE SKILLS

List your caregiver and/or life skills. These are your secret superpowers that make you amazing.

Examples: *Project managing, organizing, supporting others, hugging, baking, listening attentively, multi-tasking, counseling, strategizing college savings plans...*

Unlock Your Venn Diagram

Nice! Three brainstorming worksheets done and dusted. Did any themes emerge as you worked through the three skill sets? How often did you think of something and jump back to a previous worksheet? (Hint: that is allowed.)

Let's collate our data and draw out some new awareness.

Review your three skills worksheets and look for similarities. Find where one word emerged in multiple places.

- Do you deal with numbers in all three spaces?
- Are you a continuous learner?
- Do you coach?

Where do you see different words with similar themes?

- Do you connect with or support other people?
- How does your energy show up?
- Maybe you regularly conflict manage?

Make notes. Update and adjust the pre-work sheets as you see fit.

Now for our Venn Diagram!

Take each skill from your list and add it to the diagram on the next page. When a skill overlaps, write it in the overlap of the related circles.

Stay curious and creative as you complete this exercise. Before you plant any word firmly in a single circle, roll it over in your head—

I am excellent at defining strategies in my leadership role.

Do I ever use that to be more successful at home?

Do I work through technical projects strategically?

Chances are yes!

Transferable Skills
VENN DIAGRAM

Thoughtfully place your technical, leadership, and mom / life skills in the overlapping circles.

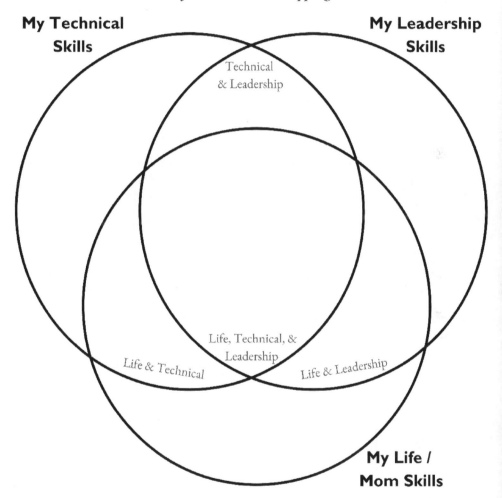

My Technical Skills

My Leadership Skills

Technical & Leadership

Life, Technical, & Leadership

Life & Technical

Life & Leadership

My Life / Mom Skills

Career Returners: *If you've taken a leave from paid work and are ready to return, this is a great way to start visualizing and embracing skills to celebrate on your next resume.*

Convert Skills into Action

In Chapter 1 we have dug deep into transferable skills. You are building an awesome toolbox to leverage throughout the day, night, weekend, and all the time in between.

When we pause and look around for a moment, we might notice that only 22.5% of all engineering bachelor's degrees awarded in America go to women today.[4] Women at the top of any organization are sparce. The term "working mom" still prevails, while you would never hear a man referred to as a "working dad."

It's not hard to see why we feel unique (or even isolated) in our quest.

Supporting Career Returners

In 2022, LinkedIn added "Stay-at-Home Mom," "Stay-at-Home Dad," and "Stay-at-Home Parent"!

Why should allies care?

The next time you're scanning through resumes and you notice a gap in education, don't throw that candidate out. Be curious, get more information.

And if the applicant was bold enough to write "stay-at-home parent," schedule them for an interview right away. They are likely to be skilled in multi-tasking, flexible, authentic, and brave.

Moreover, they'll likely be your most reliable employee. You'll learn that many working moms are in search of supportive companies where they can grow and add value.

[4] See National Center for Education Statistics (NCES). *Table 318.30. Bachelor's, master's, and doctor's degrees conferred by postsecondary institutions, by sex of student and discipline division: 2017-18.* 2019.

But this is also why our suite of skills is such a powerful differentiator. What Venn Diagram superpowers do you want to leverage today?

One last action to lock in our new love of transferable skills. Take a minute and reflect on the three lists you created and that beautifully cluttered diagram. Think of a skill you want to focus on developing, or a connection you never made before that you are proud of. Capture your thoughts in the reflection box.

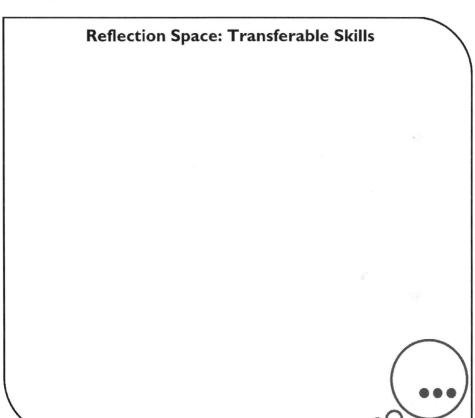

Reflection Space: Transferable Skills

For the next week, pay attention every time you use your skills. Watch how you feel. Consider:

- Are there situations where you could use a particular skill more?
- Do you use any skills more than you thought?

At the end of the week, reflect again on how it felt knowing you have superpower skills you get to develop and leverage every day.

As a parent and leader, I know how to set clear boundaries and expectations. I have learned the value of being consistent. I know never to take myself too seriously. Humility is a terrific attribute when applied well.

Of course, some skills are just for one circle in our Venn Diagrams. Being a great hugger might want to stay squarely with Mom Skills. As you reflect on your own blend of technical, leadership, and life skills, know that you are highly capable and ready to go places.

So, where do you want to go?

CHAPTER 2

SET A WINNING STRATEGY

Playing softball is a weird way to get a job offer.

Maybe not so much if you're excellent at softball, or you are aspiring to join the Women's Professional Fastpitch league. But that's not how it was for me.

In 2016 I travelled for a leadership course at the company's residential training campus. Along with interesting classes in the day and delicious food all night, recreation was encouraged. This was my third time at "leadership camp," so I decided I needed to push my comfort zone and participate in the social activities a bit more. Best option, I decided to play pickup softball with 17 random fellow middle-managers.

I'm strong at most sports, but I retired from softball back in the 5th grade after a career of silly songs from the dugout and daisy chain crafting adventures. It's not my sport.

Despite my lack of skill, the awkwardness of the social situation, and the fact there were no daisies for chaining anywhere in sight, I walked away from that game with a job offer. Not just any job offer, this was a promotion to senior management!

Know When to Say Yes

Thankfully, with the support of a generous mentor, I had already done soul searching on what I want for my own career. My husband and I had also spent significant time discussing our hopes and dreams for our shared life. I was clear about my values, and even had a crisp clean document capturing what I would be looking for in any future role. The list had ten items, so naturally I call it *My Top 10*.

When this promotion was offered to me out of the blue, it was my first chance to put my top 10 to the test! I was excited to try out this new career navigating strategy. I thoughtfully cross-referenced what I knew about the job (which honestly wasn't much) to my top 10…

The results were a no brainer—this was NOT a good opportunity. I turned it down.

Why did I reject such a good offer so quickly? See the table below with what I knew about the job at that time. If these were your goals and values, would you have taken the job?

MY TOP 10	SOFTBALL OFFER	
1. Roles where I can add value for PEOPLE at scale.	✓	Larger team, larger scale. Could be fun!
2. Products I am excited to deliver.	✓	World class aircraft to be delivered globally.
3. Time and support to mentor, connect, and coach.	?	Depends on other time commitments, but possible.
4. Part deep technical work, part big picture strategic freedom.	?	Offer is outside my technical knowledge, which means either learning from a firehose or getting stuck on oversight.

MY TOP 10	SOFTBALL OFFER	
5. Positive leadership team that extends trust.	?	Who knows! Just met my boss at happy hour softball.
6. Opportunities to learn from inspiring peers and leaders.	✓	This would be a 100% learning role, at least to start.
7. A positive day-to-day engaged team to collaborate with.	?	They're probably very nice people.
8. Flexibility in work schedule with no more than 6 business trips per year.	✗	2.5-hour commute every day (2-hours more than right now), plus lots of business travel.
9. Ability to get boys to soccer and school daily, and possibly coach.	✗	2.5-hour commute means I won't be home before 6:30 ever.
10. Mental health (positive stress is good if there is time for mental recovery too).	✗	Highly unlikely if I'm out of my technical wheelhouse, sitting in traffic for hours each day, never seeing my family, and completely removed from my professional support network.

At first, the opportunity seemed ideal. Bigger job on a globally recognized product! But when I spent the time to look at my full list (which is not in any prioritized order), the shine of the offer faded quickly. I found that only three of my top ten goals and values would be fully satisfied. Four more had potential, depending on the leadership structure and the team culture. And then there were three that would not be fulfilled at all.

That's not enough for me, or my family. I respectfully declined.

To feel like you're winning at home and at work, a good strategy is key. If I had taken the softball offer, I might have temporarily felt like I was winning at work. It's a promotion! Honestly, long term I could have learned the job by leveraging the foundation of knowledge I have. It's very possible that the team I would have joined might have had a supportive culture and dynamic leaders to learn from, like the role I was currently in.

But what would I have been trading? Family and mental health are no less important to me than amazing products.

My top 10 list is an invaluable resource I carry with me through all major life decisions. It guides my thought process to think past the bling of a big raise or title and process thoughtfully how each opportunity aligns to a broader set of personal goals and values.

I use it as a starting point. Often jobs do not score 10 out of 10, but if I see eight check marks, I know where to focus my negotiations.[1]

Define Your Personal Goals & Values

To get to your own *Top 10* list, first we need to look at the bigger picture. What do you really want?

Sounds simple enough, right?! As a working parent, answering this seemingly benign question quickly gets complicated.

---

[1] In my experience as an applicant and a hiring manager I've learned that you should negotiate at least one aspect of every job offer.

Leadership books might tell us to *chart our course, take no prisoners,* and *go big or go home!* But what if we kinda like going home?

Parenting books tell us to limit screen time and to enjoy every moment because *time goes by so fast.* They also say we need to potty train by spending a whole week at home with our kid in butts out mode, which is hard to do when you have a customer meeting on Thursday.

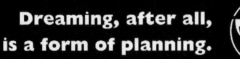 **Dreaming, after all, is a form of planning.**

Gloria Steinem

gloriasteinem.com

We are in a crazy tug of war between conflicting goals and social norms. The barrage of advice is of no help. As STEM moms, I feel we experience this juxtaposition even more keenly than most.

Our male counterparts rarely relate, even when they want to.

We are solving for multiple variables in a complex set of equations. It's not just a question of what we want to do during our days, but how do we want to connect that to our home life? How will you and your partner support each other's goals? And where do you want to merge or decouple career from home?[2]

To start solving our partial differential equations, it's time to look at a few introspective questions. They are a variation of three questions my wonderful mentor Dan asked me very early in my career. My answers have changed over time, but not as much as I thought they would.

If taken to heart, each of these can provide valuable insight into who you are and what you value.

---

[2] Please consider "partner" however it best serves you. My husband is my partner. He is the one I choose to co-create my future. Your partner might be your life partner, your best friend, or maybe your mom. Who is your person (outside of work preferably) that you seek out when making big decisions?

We will walk through the three questions individually first and then set you free on an aspirations deep dive of your own. These questions are meant to be bold and thought provoking.

If you're struggling to push your creativity, just repeat to yourself Eleanor Roosevelts wise words… "the future belongs to those who believe in the beauty of their dreams."

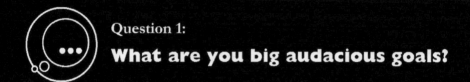

Question 1:

What are you big audacious goals?

If you could do anything, be anything, see anything, achieve anything, what would that be? Simple enough, right? The sky is not the limit here, keep going!

Go as big and as crazy as you want. If it makes you giggle or feel awkward to write it down, you're probably on the right track. This can include work goals, personal goals, goals for humanity or the universe. What excites you about your future?

Question 2:

What do you want from your career?

Imagine your future professional life. Consider:

Are there milestones you want to achieve?

Is there a title you want to earn?

What impacts do you want to create?

For another way to look at it, consider what you want people to say at your retirement party. Do you want to live on in history books, or would you prefer a few quiet handshakes for a job well done?

It could be that what you truly want from your career is a stable paycheck, or to solve global warming. You can be specific or broad, fantastic or practical—or both!

Invest some time thinking about what in your career excites you. What do you want to accomplish with all this time you are investing in your day job?

Question 3:
What does "work-life balance" mean to you?

Here's the kicker. This is the most personal of the questions, and I'll wager your answer will be at least slightly different from every other mom in STEM.

Think it through—mull it over. There are no right or wrong answers.

Many different forms of the term "work-life balance" have surfaced over recent years; work-life integration, work-life blend, harmony... all nice words, but when it comes to it, all that matters is what you want it to be.

We're not looking for an essay on the morals of being a working parent, or how much people will judge you if you're not the one picking your kids up from school. Leave all the guilt at the door.

What day-to-day changes would mean more balance (or harmony...) for you? What in your personal life feeds you energy? What about in your career? Is there any way these energizers can connect and support one and other?

Now it's your turn!

Grab a cup of coffee, or an adult beverage, and enjoy some quiet time contemplating these three aspiration-focused questions. When you're ready, capture your thoughts on the next page.

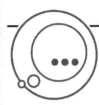

Aspirations Deep Dive

Capture your thoughts using the space below.

1 **What are your big audacious goals?**

2 **What do you want from your career?**

3 **What does "work-life balance" mean to you?**

And then celebrate! Take a moment, step back, and soak in the honest thoughts you just shared with yourself. We are making progress toward your top 10 list. Your big picture is becoming clearer. Next step is to translate the answers above into goals and values.

Do you see clear actionable goals floating out of the deep dive? You might already see plans falling into place to complete a worthy task, or the start of a new goal you would like to investigate further.

Goals are typically quantifiable in nature. A well-defined goal is usually specific, measurable, achievable, relevant, and time-bound (SMART). Maybe you've been asked to set annual professional goals using SMART before.

In our personal lives we set New Year's goals (aka resolutions) to work out more or cut back on spending. We bind the effort to the next year, we promise ourselves it's doable, and we might even download a new app to measure our progress.

Finding Mentoring Partnerships

Leaders and allies, the aspirations deep dive activity can also be an incredibly useful tool to connect with people you are supporting.

Consider sharing these questions with potential mentees. You will learn so much about that person, and how you can create the most value for them in your partnership.

The questions can also help determine if you two are a strong mentoring match. If your potential mentee says they want to be the CEO within the decade, and you are much more excited about your role as a technical expert, you might want to help them find a business minded mentor.

Then again, if your life goals align, or if you just "click," you might choose to join their support network anyway.
We all need champions.

Goals are powerful, especially for analytically-minded individuals, because we can track them. We know how we're doing and can see when we need to adjust.

Values, on the other hand, are abstract. They are our North Star, guiding us in every decision we make to stay true to our beliefs. Values are rarely measurable, highly unlikely to be time-bound, and occasionally they are even irrelevant. They are often phrased as qualities or states of being rather than verbs.

Here are a few examples of the multitude of personal values people in this world hold:

Vivacity	Understanding
Authenticity	Excellence
Love	Strength[3]

Looking back at your deep dive, do you see values woven throughout? The first time I worked through each question I discovered the start of many goals which I have since iterated on to form the following:

- I want to show up for all my kids' soccer games.
- I want to grow women and moms in STEM.
- I want to go on adventures.
- I want international work assignments.

My personal values also surfaced:

Adventure	Balance
Effort	Fortitude
Resilience	Self-Improvement...

Grab some highlighters or colored pencils and go back through your answers. What themes do you see? What values stand out? Capture your thoughts on your personal goals and values in the reflection box provided on the next page.

---

[3] See what I did there?

Reflection Space: Goals & Values

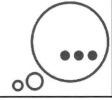

Share Your Values

While it's amazing to have clarity on your personal big audacious goals and North Star, we still have more variables to solve for when we're on a team.

Are you willing to share your goals and values with your partner or support team? Would it be valuable to learn about their goals and values too? Consider inviting the person or people you care about to work through the same activity.

Years ago, my husband and I defined our own values by considering what defines us and makes us slightly quirky. We get eye rolls when we talk about sports; we spend a lot of our free time racing in muddy parks (#cyclocross) or dressing in fleece lined leggings for winter beach volleyball. We receive similar levels of loving mockery from friends regarding how we approach continuous learning, our commitment to family (both biological and chosen), the time we dedicate to adventure, and how we protect all the above through smart investments as we go.

After many deep conversations, we decided our six most relevant family-defining values are:

Education
Family
Friendships
Fun
Fitness
Financial Security... or EFFFFF-it for short. [1]

To know what you want to do, it's good to know what your home team needs too.[2] Whatever you come up with together will be a solid start. Honestly, I felt the conversation was more important than the words that came out at the end.

From this point forward, you will have increased confidence that large decisions you make are in alignment with your favorite support system.

Does this mean when you get an international job offer, you get to say yes immediately?

Probably not. Life changing commitments deserve a second conversation.

If you and your partner decided you really do value adventure though, you can start opening the aperture of international opportunities. That might mean telling anyone who will listen (bosses, mentors, HR, that woman who just came back from Bengalūru...) about your interests. Or it might mean you start applying to every job that pops up on LinkedIn. The important thing is you now have clarity and alignment, which means you can start making value-aligned decisions.

Design Home Team Goals

With clarity on values in hand, what if you and your home team were actively aligned on what you want to do (aka accomplish) today, tomorrow, or the rest of this year?

---

[1] We followed Patrick Lencioni's framework to establish our values. If you would like a more detailed approach to establishing your own values, see *The Three Big Questions for the Frantic Family: A Leadership Fable...About Restoring Sanity to the Most Important Organization in Your Life.* San Francisco: Jossey-Bass, 2008.

[2] Please consider "home team" as your team outside of work. I chose to use home in lieu of family as parenthood and caregiving have so many permutations.

Traditionally, New Year's Eve is a time to resolve. Most people think about what they did in the past and promise to make change next year. Sometimes these resolutions stick—sometimes they don't. Either way, I believe the gym industry appreciates the January surge.

Several years ago, I decided to make a pivot from this tradition. I wanted to look forward to the abundance of time coming in the next year. The new year is a full 365.25 days of opportunity!

I cracked a bottle of bubbly with my husband, grabbed an old chalkboard, and started listing out all the things we wanted to do the following year. Together we identified personal goals, family goals, vacations we'd dreamed of, and friends we wanted to see.

The result, we had a most fabulous year! We proudly hung the chalkboard in the kitchen, and on cold rainy Wednesdays we would look at it and say, "Oh yeah, we did want to go visit my aunt in the desert. Let's do that this weekend."

The year was more focused. Without taking anything away from my professional pursuits, it added direction and fulfillment to our home life.

It worked well for a couple key reasons.

1) We wrote it down.
2) We kept it light.

As I've heard so many times throughout my professional career, what gets measured gets done. There is a reason corporations live off metrics. By bringing attention to something, it indicates importance. And people like to work on important things.

I'm not proposing you start creating detailed metrics for your annual chalkboard. Please do not schedule quarterly performance reviews at the kitchen table. That would be going against the second key reason— keep it light. But what if you had a simple visual reminder in your kitchen or mudroom?

This is where the YOLO chalkboard shines.

Through the years our chalkboard has grown to be a treasured annual activity. Our kids now add their goals and insist on helping write directly on the board (which just kills the neat freak in me, but I'm trying my best to remind myself this is just for fun).

Many of our friends and extended family have taken up the tradition as well. One family makes multiple columns each year with specific and measurable (SMART) goals for each person separately, and then another column for their combined adventures.

A highly organized friend chose to use a whiteboard because chalk is too messy. Another couple lists destinations they dream of visiting. Nothing else.

One dear friend shared they had hung their board visibly in the kitchen last year (as it is a great conversation starter), but secretly wrote "get pregnant" on the back side just for the two of them to know and cherish.

To each their own.

Keep it playful. Keep it simple. And don't be too hard on yourself when the year takes a crazy turn, and you only cross off seven of the 30 ideas. It is a prompt, not a rule book. Our house rule is not every goal should be achievable. We always include some extra audacious ideas.

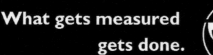

What gets measured gets done.

Nearly every manager ever.[3]

The main thing is to embrace a "you only live once" (YOLO) mentality. This is your year, enjoy it. Use the guide on the next page as a starting point for you and your home team to craft your own YOLO chalkboard.

---

[3] The phrase "what gets measured gets done" is often attributed to Peter Drucker, renowned management consultant circa 1942. However, there is no evidence that he ever said it. The earliest known appearance of the phrase is in a 1951 article by V.F. Ridgway, titled "Dysfunctional Consequences of Performance Measurements." (Ridgway, 1951).

Group Activity
YOLO CHALKBOARD

Make this year memorable by planning goals with your home team. Make them as measurable or broad as you like.

Step 1: Brainstorm big ideas for the rest of this year with your favorite people.

Step 2: Make a single list and display it proudly.

Include:
- Your personal goals.
- Your partner's and/or home team member's goals.
- Combined / group goals.

Suggestions:
- Use chalk or dry erase markers so it doesn't feel set in stone.
- Check in with your aspirations deep dive answers for inspiration. Encourage your home team to do the same.
- Be brief. This is a quick reference reminder, not a step-by-step execution plan.
- Cross off goals you accomplish.
- Keep it fun and positive!

Step 3: Make a plan to revisit on New Year's Eve!

Stay Flexible: December 31, 2020, was a curious moment. Vaccines were just starting to come out; my kids were still at home. We chose to only fill in half our board that night. We added more throughout the year as we gained clarity on what was and was not possible.

Know What You Want

Checking in. How does this all feel?

If you've been working through the exercises, you are gaining clarity on your goals and values. You have a strategy to make this year a year to remember, and you either have, or have a plan to, connect with your home team to tie it all together.

It's time to start translating all this wonderful work you've been doing into one more tangible, actionable artifact… your very own top 10 list. It will be your very own tool to thoughtfully navigate life's toughest decision points.

At the beginning of Chapter 2 I shared my top 10 list. It is the tool I leveraged to decide if I wanted to trade my beautifully short commute and role I loved for a promotion. This tool, or framework, has lived with me for many years. It has evolved and changed as I have grown myself.

In the softball example I did not take the job. In many other situations I took opportunities with open arms. My top 10 has helped when I had multiple options to choose from. It has also helped me when I had no opportunities, but I knew I needed a change because my current role no longer brought me energy. It is my companion and a catalyst to go out and seek new opportunities.

In all its various forms and applications, my top 10 list has been an incredible tool.

At its core, your top 10 will be a list of what you are looking for in any job. These can be personal, professional, financial, superficial, whatever you in your heart of hearts really are excited by.[4]

If you know exactly what you want in your own top 10, feel free to jump forward to page 52, and have fun!

---

[4] Shoutout to my mentor Kristin Robertson who first encouraged me to write down the ten things I was looking for in my next job.

If you want a bit more support to ensure you are connecting all that effort you just did on goals and vision, let's do just a bit more prep work by answering the six W questions…

Like any good elementary school research paper, start with the basics: who, what, where, when, why, and how.

Consider:

Who do you enjoy working with? Your answer could be specific names or traits of leaders and peers you tend to feel energized by.

What past jobs have excited you? What roles do you dream of trying?

Where do you want to spend your time? Do you want to work from home, in an office environment, or hybrid? Do you want to travel a lot and see the world? Do you want international adventures? Do you want people to stop asking you to get out of your pajamas because you work just fine from your couch?

When do you want to be available to work? When do you not? How long each day do you want to be working? When do you want to retire? take a sabbatical? switch to full-time?

Why do you work? What motivates you to spend 2080+ hours a year digging in and doing what you do best? This is the time to look back at the rest of your thoughts from that second aspirational question.

And finally…

How do you want to show up? How do you want others to think about you?

For bonus points, consider other leaders or peers you have come across who have inspired you. What about how they showed up do you want to emulate? What can you take and improve on?

The worksheet on the next two pages is for you to brainstorm your six W questions. Take a sip of coffee and dive in.

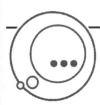

Top 10 Pre-Work
SIX Ws

1 **WHO** do you enjoy working with?

2 **WHAT** roles do you dream of trying?

3 **WHERE** do you want to spend your time?

4 **WHEN do you want to be available to work?**

5 **WHY do you work?**

6 **HOW do you want to show up?**

Now it's time to scribble all over this pre-work in pursuit of our top 10. Grab another color and start underlining words and phrases that resonate for you. Highlight the thoughts that naturally burst from your pen even before you realized you had a fully articulated thought.

Focus on the ideas, wants, and needs that are important for any role you take going forward. After you're done, count the items you marked.

If you highlighted:

1-5 Ideas

Consider if there is a second layer of interesting thoughts you could add.

6-14 Ideas

Consider each item and why it's meaningful to you. Iterate to refine and clarify in alignment with your values. Consolidate or expand only as applicable to your personal needs. Play with phrasing.

15+ Ideas

Consider if there are recurring themes. If ideas don't merge easily, which subset of this list out-prioritizes the others. If it's all critical, keep it. This is your list!

I have found through my iterations that very broad statements do not help me when it comes to making decisions.

For example:

- I agree that "making money" is a reason we work, but how much money? Is there a quality of life you want to achieve through some threshold of salary?
- "Save the world" is noble. Would you be equally excited to work alongside Dr. Jane Goodall or Melinda French Gates? Both are fantastically inspiring STEM moms, but if you have a preference, articulate it.

I have also found being overly specific can be constraining:

- "Finite Element Modelling using Nastran to post-process" might be more useful if written as "Opportunity for detailed structural analysis with tools I love or can learn quickly."

After a few iterations (design, build, test), you will be close to a list of 7 to 12 key items, concepts, phrases, etc. you want in any job. When you're ready, transfer your ideas onto the next page. Choose any order that suits you. No pressure, this is a first draft.

I highly recommend typing this up. Save it somewhere accessible to pull up at any moment. You never know when opportunity will knock.[5]

The greatest value of this top 10 (or 7 or 11) list is that it is your own. It is a tool aligned to your personal values and goals. When completed and leveraged thoughtfully, it is a compass to guide you in making any decision.

---

[5] Simple Life Hack: I have a folder called "Career Development" on my desktop where I also saved versions of my resumes, bios, professional photos, and a colorful slide with my answers to the audacious questions.

My Top 10 List
WHAT I WANT IN ANY JOB

*List what's most important to you when choosing
any professional next step.*

Iterate: *Use this list to empower your career and life as you
press forward on your adventure. Consider it a draft to be
revisited as needed.*

Bring Goals to Life

We aspire to feel like we're winning in life. We want to know we are dedicating our precious time toward what we care most about, both personally and professionally.

In Chapter 2 we have gone deep into who we are, what excites us, what is important. You are now equipped with your own personal toolbox to help you navigate any major decision.

Well done for investing your time and energy to create your own personal goals and values. And extra credit if you engaged your home team too.

You can now have more confidence that every decision you make will aid in your quest for balance and personal satisfaction. You can let go of external pressures and social norms, opting for the pursuit of what is right for you and your people.

Next, we'll look at career progression in more detail. Remember that your top 10 list is only a starting point. We have a bit more to consider regarding what makes a job "right."

Keep your aspirations deep dive close. They will be guides as we look more specifically into how to actively navigate personal and professional growth as you design your best life.

CHAPTER 3

CREATE POSITIVE CHANGE

Sometimes something's gotta give.

I've had many people explain the three-legged stool to me in subtly different permutations.

"You see it's like a three-legged stool," they often start. They then go on to explain balance as though the elementary theory of three points making a mathematical plane is the same as my personal journey of iteratively solving for the infinite variables of life as a mom, engineer, leader, and human.

In this metaphor, the hypothetical legs of the stool sometimes change, but it is typically some version of balancing family, career, and selfcare or health. At one point I nearly bought into it. This must be the secret solution to success!

And then my own mom got sick.

At the time, I was recently promoted. I had just chosen to transfer off the program I had grown up on. I was jumping into a new technical domain, systems engineering, rather than my oh so comfortable mechanical design.

Despite program pressures, I chose to travel north weekly to support my dad who was suddenly my mom's fulltime caregiver. This meant I missed a full day in the office each week. Again, my choice. I prioritized weekend days with my husband and kids over facetime with coworkers.

I don't know what I was trying to stand on, but it was definitely not a neatly balanced stool.

Work assured me they were supportive, but as the program's challenges increased, the senior integration leader (that's me) was expected to be present. I worked my hours, but in four days rather than five. This extended the time between daycare drop-offs and pick-ups, so I doubled down on my availability for quality time at home.

The family leg quickly fractured into three pieces: my spouse, my family unit (husband + kids), and my extended family. The career leg started squeaking, despite my best efforts to play it cool. I couldn't find the self-care leg anywhere.

I do not regret for one second the time I spent supporting my parents. It was incredibly hard though, and it reminded me that even the best laid plans are unstable. Balance is not a badge you can collect, wrap in a nice container, and tuck in your pocket to keep safe forever.

In Chapter 3 we are going to get into strategies to set ourselves up for success even when we've misplaced our Balance Badge, or the days when we consciously choose to trade it in for a while.

I'll be offering a framework for considering the level of support any career transition will require, which is highly dependent on how far you are extending your comfort zone with each step. To know where you want to step, we're also going to do some hands-on work with long term career planning.

Grow Thoughtfully

While we may not be able to create success-assured balance forever, we can make conscientious decisions now to support our future selves when the going gets tough.

Opportunities will come. How are you going to decipher which opportunities are good, which are bad, and which ones might be good but you're not sure if you'll have the resources you need if/when it all hits the fan?

You already know the first part of the answer—cross check the offer with your top 10 list. Easy-peasy. However, while your top 10 list aligns to your aspirations and passions, it might sometimes inspire you to jump in headfirst.

Taking one more thoughtful step before you say, "Yes, I can start today!" can shed some light on how far you are stretching yourself, and how much support you will have along the way.

This step is a quick review of the Technical vs. Leadership Growth Grid, which addresses where you are now and considers the size of the growth you are considering taking on in both your technical depth and leadership skills.

The elevator to success is broken. Take the stairs. Jenifer Lewis[1]

The grid on the next page is a seemingly simple graphic. It is an X and Y axis with a grand total of 4 quadrants. However, it is an incredibly powerful resource when applied well. [2]

---

[1] See "Jenifer Lewis gives powerful speech at Baggage Claim premiere," on YouTube, TrueExclusives. September 20, 2013.

[2] Shoutout to my mentor Jamie Burgess who first shared with me technical versus leadership growth in the framework of an X-Y graph, which he literally drew on the back of an old envelope.

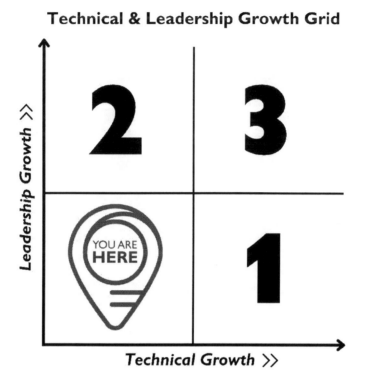

Technical & Leadership Growth Grid

Any time you have an opportunity for professional change, visualize yourself in the bottom left quadrant. From here, you can choose to expand your technical skills (Option 1), or your leadership skills (Option 2), or both (Option 3).

When you took your first position straight out of college, you were leaping into a new business with new products (and acronyms) to learn. It is unlikely you were expected to also lead a team, change was (or soon will be if you're in college today) primarily a technical growth opportunity—aka Option 1.

The next step might have been a few years later to another product team or research project. Hypothetically, you took a role that pushed your technical depth or expanded your technical breadth.

This is Option 1 again.

At some point in the theoretical profession journey, your proactive attitude and ability to learn quickly made you stand out, and you were asked to take on a project lead role within your team. It's the same product and technical scope, but now you are learning how to task other people, and maybe sharpening your project management skills. This is leadership growth—Option 2.

Following this format, you might imagine your entire career as a massive flight of stairs. Some steps are a wide series of technical growth opportunities that move you forward with momentum. Others lift you up toward your leadership goals.

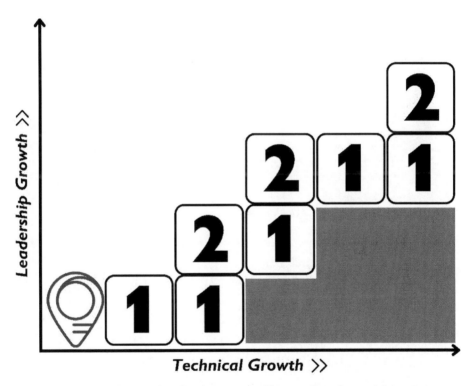

Each step up or forward will take some effort at first, but with each you will learn and grow. It takes work and tenacity. By putting in the work, accomplishing hard things, and then advancing, you are creating a strong foundation for success.

Your hard work will earn you additional skills and experiences that you can call back to when you are problem solving your industry's toughest challenges with grace and power.

But what about Option 3?

Option 3 opportunities will come, or you might seek them out. Take for example my time on that development program. I had switched from mechanical design to systems engineering (technical growth). I also moved from a first line manager to a senior manager. It was my first experience with managers reporting to me (leadership growth). That double shift experience had the potential to be an amazing career booster, if I had considered a few more important details.

Support Structure:

Who is your extended network of support in this new position? Consider if those around you will be cheering for you, and offering support when you need it.

Technical Growth Mentor:

Do you have a technical expert that can actively coach you in the first months? If you are extending yourself in two directions at once, this person is key to accelerating your learning.

Leadership Growth Mentor:

Who is going to be your sounding board for leadership challenges? Whether it's one person, your manager, or a small but trusted peer group, having people to talk to about all the weird things that come up when you start leading others will help with stress management and sanity. I find especially in highly structured management chains, having trusted support at your level or higher is critical for the tougher days.

Option 3 career moves can be exciting. They have the power to accelerate careers in surprising ways. Using the network ideas above, you can make this leap a resounding success for your career and your personal growth.

My step into senior management was a bold Option 3 move. Unfortunately, while I had some support from people who had moved programs with me, I did not spend enough time building my technical and leadership mentor partnerships in advance. When other variables in my life took a dramatic turn, my balance suffered.

Thankfully, we are resilient, and even the most challenging times offer new opportunities. I learned, I adjusted, and I built partnerships on the fly. The next move I made in my career was an Option 1—new technical domain, same leadership level. I moved to a team where people were cheering for me even before I walked through the door. I set up weekly meetings with my new manager to build camaraderie. And I quickly learned who my go-to technical experts were and built trust.

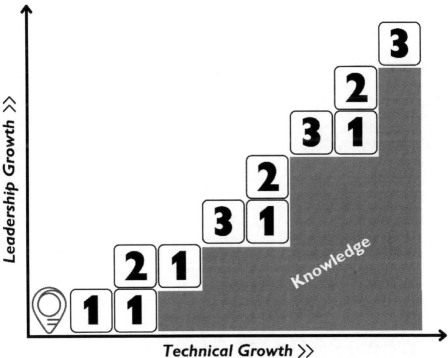

There is no perfect code for the best career, only the career that works best for you. My career looked a lot like 1-1-2-1-3-1-2-3-1-2-3... but that's just me. Choose how often you want to leap, and when you need controlled growth. Build your support network and enjoy the climb.

And remember, every step forward and up builds your foundation of knowledge, making you more skilled and able to continue your professional growth!

Returning to our four-quadrant visual, let's add some space to remember the importance of a support network. Consider this expanded supported technical and leadership growth grid. The new column is offered as a brainstorming space to remember who is in your corner right now, and as a prompt to plan for where you need to foster new relationships.

Supported Technical & Leadership Growth Grid

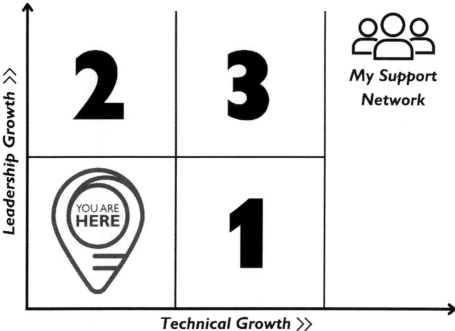

As you take that next step, set yourself up for success by planning where you will find support. Every job can be a fabulous opportunity when you understand the extent of growth and move forward with your eyes wide open.

With this new tool in hand, let's dive deep into the career moves you want to make, and why!

Proactively Move Toward Your Best Life

I have no interest in clearly seeing all the twists and turns of my future. Prophets never seem to live the best of lives—poor Cassandra of Troy, poor Bruno.

Rather than being over-confident that we know our future, only to feel rattled when it all suddenly changes, what would happen if we apply our design, build, test model? Could an iterative mindset ease anxiety over the future and possibly allow the process of making life decisions to be more enjoyable?

You have likely been encouraged to write a 5 year plan at some point in your own career. The idea is to lay out exactly what you want to do for the next five years, and then go do it. Simple and actionable. Invest ten minutes and you'll have clarity for the next half decade.

If you have gone through this activity before, did you check back five years later to see how accurate your plan was?

I have made several 5 year plans, and they always bring me a good laugh later. I was going to have kids at 28 and 32, but got eager and had them at 27 and 30 instead. I was going to go for my first management role in 4 years, but the perfect opportunity (with a strong network of support) came up after one year, so I went for it!

Life is dynamic. It is sticky. It involves making hard choices and dealing with change you never saw coming. It can also be better than you allowed yourself to imagine and it can move much faster than a one-page plan could ever foresee.

So rather than a static plan, let's look at building a set of flexible and fun maps—versions of lives where we make different choices aligned in different ways to our goals and values.

Image that you are going to actively and wholeheartedly pursue your biggest, craziest goals. How would that feel?

Could you create that reality?

Let's review the aspirations deep dive questions from Chapter 1:

1 **What are your big audacious goals?**

2 **What do you want from your career?**

3 **What does "work-life balance" mean to you?**

Your answers to these three questions might included several markers you will want to include on the maps you will build later in this section.

To keep things simple, we're going to break these three questions down one at a time.

Identify Your Most Audacious Map Markers

First up are your big audacious goals! On the next page you will find a worksheet that walks through your goals then asks you what events, accomplishments, milestones, time investments, etc., you would need to add to your life plan to reach those goals. Sticking with the map theme, we're calling these inflection points *markers*. They are the actions you take in your own life—mileposts of effort.

Once you have the super high-level road signs in place, shift your focus to the near term. In the next days, weeks, months, or maybe a year, what progress could you make toward each goal?

Write it all down. Don't allow yourself to be limited by constraints right now, only focus on your goals and actions that will move you closer to those goals.

Remember, you are allowed to go even bigger on your goals than what you wrote in Chapter 1. This is your time to reach for the moon.

5 Year Maps Pre-Work
AUDACIOUS MAP MARKERS

What are your big audacious goals?
Rewrite or revise/iterate on your deep dive thoughts.

What big-picture actions could turn your goal into reality?

Examples: Earn a teaching certificate, get elected, enroll in flight school, quit my job...

What are near-term actions you can take to get started?

Examples: Graduate, apply for management, volunteer, retire...

Identify Your Fulfilling Career Map Markers

Now jump forward to the day you are retiring…

Congratulations, you put in so much hard work and accomplished so much. Have some cake!

As you eat that delicious lemon cake with home-made frosting, what memories from your journey to this point do you want to cherish? Do you want to be proud of a certain title you achieved or a scientific discovery that cured some horrible disease? Do you want to be famous? (If yes, add a few cameras and a news crew to this memory of yours).

Who do you want to be at your retirement party (other than that news team)? Do the people you hope to celebrate this accomplishment with change how you want to get there?

Use this future imagery to enhance your previous answer to the aspirational career question. Write your new answer on the next page's worksheet. Elaborate as much as possible.

Similar to the audacious goals activity, what mile-markers in your career will help you reach this desired end-state?

Then again, shifting to the near term, how can you get started? Or maybe you're already on your way and you only need one or two course corrections. In the next days, weeks, months, and years, what progress could you make toward this manifested success story?

This could be a Master's program you want to apply for or shadowing that leader you respect who keeps offering to spend a day with you. You may want to start teaching or mentoring others. Possibly your biggest career goals are well within hand, and you want to spend your time creating value for others. Absolutely no wrong answers here.

Write it all down—this is all for you.

5 Year Maps Pre-Work
CAREER MAP MARKERS

What do you want from your career?
Rewrite or revise/iterate on your deep dive thoughts.

What big-picture actions will support your career goals?

Examples: Promotions, education, mentors, deliverables, wins...

What are near-term actions you can take to get started?

Examples: Learn Java, enroll in night school, go to a conference, tweet...

Identify Your Best Life's Map Markers

You spent a lot of time on professional life over the last two worksheets. But as a STEM mom, you know there is so much more to this puzzle.

Now we get to weave it all back together. In Chapter 1's deep dive we thought about what work-life balance is. Here we're going to deviate slightly. We're now going to ponder how we want to live our best life. It could be integrated, balanced, totally askew, or compartmentalized to the max.

What major life moments do you want in your own highly personal and completely outstanding life story?

You might already be super clear on this, or this could be a list of a few hypotheticals… either's fine. Take some time with these questions and see if you can dig even deeper.

This is your life; how do you want to live it?

Use the third and final map markers worksheet on the next page to capture your thoughts on your most fulfilling life. I kept the examples here short. I don't want to hamper your creative flow with my personal bias—happy brainstorming!

5 Year Maps Pre-Work
FULFILLING LIFE
MAP MARKERS

What life moments do you want to experience?

What big-picture actions will help bring those experiences to life?

What are near-term actions you can take to get started?

Examples: Get a passport, build a chicken coop...

Play with Markers

Now we get to play with markers! With the time you just invested, you now have a list of career and personal milestones (aka markers) that will enable you to visualize various versions of your life. It's time to build four distinctly different versions of your future—steady-state, thoughtful, bold, and crazy.

The following worksheets are your opportunity to explore how those markers might flow through time. Each of the upcoming maps has a different theme to spark a different set of thoughts and emotions.

Steady-State:

Sit with your markers and strategize. Can you make progress on the path you are on today. If you keep pressing forward, how do you see yourself advancing over the next several years?

Thoughtful:

Sit with your markers and strategize. Can you make progress on all three sets of aspirations? Capture how this reality would play out on your map.

Bold:

What happens when you push yourself toward all your hopes and dreams? Where would you go? What would you do?

Crazy:

"We're going ballistic, Mav!" Throw all logic out the window. Map out a most extreme adventure!

Ready to get going? Tackle the four maps in whatever order most excites you! If one is not interesting to you, skip it or rename it.

The worksheets have a non-linear time axis, and that's about it. Add your major life events in the space provided. The first years consume more of the worksheet since actions are easier to plan. As time moves out, make the goals bigger and more abstract. No dates required.

Like our transferable skills activity, a change of music for each map might help. Maybe "Wrecking Ball" for that crazy map? First, here are two samples to give you a flavor of how different hypothetical STEM moms might approach this process. These samples are offered as examples only. Please don't let them limit your own creativity.

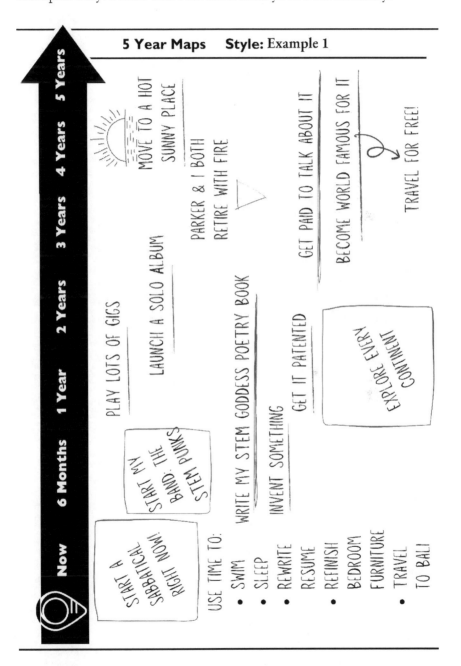

5 Year Maps   Style: Example 1

Now   6 Months   1 Year   2 Years   3 Years   4 Years   5 Years

START A SABBATICAL RIGHT NOW!

USE TIME TO:
- SWIM
- SLEEP
- REWRITE RESUME
- REFINISH BEDROOM FURNITURE
- TRAVEL TO BALI

START MY BAND: THE STEM PUNKS

PLAY LOTS OF GIGS

LAUNCH A SOLO ALBUM

WRITE MY STEM GODDESS POETRY BOOK

INVENT SOMETHING

GET IT PATENTED

EXPLORE EVERY CONTINENT

MOVE TO A HOT SUNNY PLACE

PARKER & I BOTH RETIRE WITH FIRE

GET PAID TO TALK ABOUT IT

BECOME WORLD FAMOUS FOR IT

TRAVEL FOR FREE!

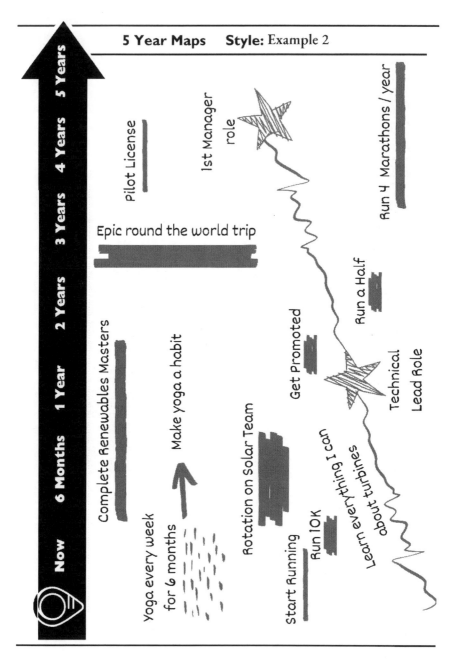

5 Year Maps   Style: Example 2

Now | 6 Months | 1 Year | 2 Years | 3 Years | 4 Years | 5 Years

Pilot License

1st Manager role

Run 4 Marathons / year

Epic round the world trip

Complete Renewables Masters

Make yoga a habit

Run a Half

Get Promoted

Technical Lead Role

Rotation on Solar Team

Learn everything I can about turbines

Yoga every week for 6 months

Start Running

Run 10K

Your turn! Turn the book sideways, and use your colored pencils, markers, protractors, whatever.

5 Year Maps   **Style:** Steady State

5 Years

4 Years

3 Years

2 Years

1 Year

6 Months

Now

5 Year Maps   **Style:** Thoughtful

5 Years

4 Years

3 Years

2 Years

1 Year

6 Months

Now

5 Year Maps   **Style:** Bold

5 Years

4 Years

3 Years

2 Years

1 Year

6 Months

Now

5 Year Maps   **Style:** Crazy

5 Years

4 Years

3 Years

2 Years

1 Year

6 Months

Now

Check in with Your Gut

I hope you found the exercise enlightening. Well done for investing the time in yourself. By avoiding thoughtful planning, we run the risk of stepping through life with the best of intentions but no clear direction.

Like our YOLO chalkboard, we are translating our intention into direction and gaining insight into what actions will serve us going forward.

> **Instinct is a marvelous thing... it can neither be explained nor ignored.**
>
> **Agatha Christie**
> *The Mysterious Affair at Styles*

Now comes the fun part! (And you thought the colored pencils were fun…)

We are going to check in with how all this planning is sitting. Find a quiet safe space with as few distractions as possible. Silence your phone, shut your office door. It's time to conduct a highly scientific *gut check*.

As a pragmatic scientist who has invested tens to hundreds of thousands of dollars in a degree from an institution that champions data driven logic, you might wonder about the value of your gut's intuition.

Turns out, our guts are a lot more insightful than you might have thought.

Somatic markers, also known as *gut feelings*, are the perceptible and imperceptible physical changes brought about by one's experience during an event. It's the prickle on the back of your neck that motivates you to get out of there quick. It's the sinking feeling in the pit of your stomach when you realize you messed up.

These somatic markers are an evolutionary tool to help us make decisions quickly (*Run! That thing has teeth!*).

Today, with a little bit of practice tuning in, they can be incredibly useful for both current and future decision making—no saber-tooths required.[3]

---

[3] See The Decision Lab. "Somatic marker hypothesis." theDecisionLab.com. 2023.

When your heart rate accelerates, you are being offered a valuable glimpse into your own perceptions. When your brow furrows, note that response. Shoulders relax and a smile spread over your face—noted.

To test this scientific phenomenon, go back to your first map. Read through it, detail by detail. Check in on how you feel as you look at the potential adventure you charted. Do you feel light or heavy? Anxious or calm? Scared, excited, or both?

Check in on your posture too. Did you naturally sit up a bit straighter, or did you slouch down and cross your arms? What are your eyebrows doing?

Listen to your instincts and capture them verbatim. Don't try to tailor or downplay here. As Agatha Christie wisely noted, we cannot explain our instincts. We can study them though.

Collect your new scientific data points with the following table. Repeat the gut check with each of your maps.

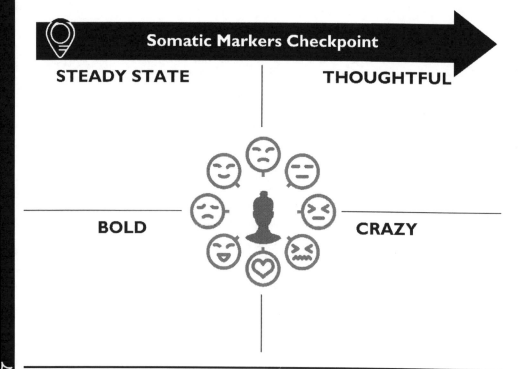

Now we have data. Maybe this feels a bit more scientific?

A gut check should not be considered conclusive evidence that one map is *wrong* and another is *right*. Staying with our iterative design, build, test mindset—all four maps have some level of right and some details that might need to be worked out as you move forward.

The ability to recognize and understand physical responses as a future planning tool is a continuous journey in developing our emotional intelligence (aka EQ). It is data though, and if applied well, this data can be very useful in planning your next steps.[4]

So, based on your somatic markers data log, what is your plan from here? Are you going to take one of your maps and run? Or will you embrace all four maps as metaphorical scaffolding to support future-you, allowing each to drive proactive change?

The first time I wrote four maps and checked my gut, I was dumbfounded. I hadn't realized how strongly I wanted to move from program leadership to people development. My steady state map had clear negative somatic markers—my shoulders rolled in and my jaw clenched. I realized I felt sad just looking at it.

My other three maps lifted me up with varying levels of grins, nervous laughs, and deep sighs. I could feel my excitement building.

I did not stay with any of the four maps verbatim, but I did iterate. It has been over a year since I first made my maps. I have changed careers from engineering manager to business owner and executive coach. It has been a bold and often crazy adventure. And I love it! Even though my changes feel extreme, I know I am making choices aligned with my goals of growing women and mothers in STEM while spending more time on self-care and with my kiddos.

It's probably time for me to check back in on my maps. Mark your calendar for a year from today and you can do the same.

---

[4] For more on emotional intelligence (EQ), see Travis Bradbury, and Jean Greaves. *Emotional Intelligence 2.0*. San Diego: TalentSmart, 2009.

Iterate on Positive Changes

The value of a map is rarely a single point destination. If it was, your phone app would not include a "find coffee along the way" button. Really, it wouldn't need to show you anything but the list of turns. But where's the adventure in that?

Embracing a charted direction keeps us moving forward toward our favorite goals. Considering how far we are stretching as we make each move helps us prepare for the challenges ahead with eyes wide open. Building a network of people we trust gives us strength to leap farther and grow faster.

Big picture clarity—check!

In Chapter 3 we have looked at when to make a move and when to keep building networks and skills to enable future successes. We have charted a plethora of exciting course options to move us toward our big audacious goals. And we have leveraged the scientifically proven wisdom of our gut to clarify intent.

If I had taken time to correlate my personal goals with my career moves, I probably would not have moved to that new development program. I had huge growth potential on my current program, an awesome support network, deep technical depth, and opportunities for continuous learning. Unfortunately, I chose to move because of the age-old wisdom, "I probably should."

My three-legged stool took a serious hit, as did my sleep routine. Fortunately, every new experience is a learning opportunity. I got smarter by becoming more intentional in my decision making for the next move and every move after. We can choose positive changes that push us, inspire us, and support us. We just need to stay flexible and proactively seek them out.

In Chapter 4 we'll dig deeper into all the joy and turmoil that comes with any adventure worth embarking on. We'll focus on day-to-day skills to help you flourish and some tools for cutting yourself slack on the days you don't.

CHAPTER 4

ROCK TODAY

Large-scale career changes might best be described as beautifully annoying explosions in an otherwise thoughtfully curated life.

I was so fortunate to sit next to Michele Campbell early in my career. She is a brilliant structural engineer and a mother making it work day-by-day. In addition to mentoring me on the fundamentals of flight test data correlation, she would often share her thoughts on life as a STEM mom. She chose one fine gray Seattle day, probably when I was considering buying a house, to caution me on the right number of transitions to target in a single year.

"Three transitions in a year is good," she said thoughtfully. "Anything more than that is too stressful. Anything less and you might get bored." She clarified that a transition is any significant change or major event, planned or unplanned.

I have played with this concept year after year, monitoring how many transitions I've had, and what even counts as a transition. In my own life I can think of several really big changes that, while mainly voluntary, yielded some new stress:

- First *real* job.
- Moved to a different country.

- Got pregnant.
- Moved to a new state.
- Pregnant again.
- Congrats, you get a second team to manage!
- Mom got sick.
- Global pandemic.
- Quit corporate life.

And some smaller but still impactful changes:

- Bought our first house.
- First kid started kindergarten.
- Trained for a half-marathon.
- Moved to a new program.
- My mentor left the company.
- Got promoted.

Some transitions are positive, some are not. Some are self-directed, and sometimes a transition jumps up and smacks you in the face without warning. I'm still honing in on my *right number* of transitions. Perhaps it should change depending on our phase of life.

Consider a year in the life of a college freshman who manages to land the out-of-state summer internship of her dreams. Her year might include upwards of 20 relatively large changes:

- 4 quarters of new classes, professors, and timetables.
- 0 to 5+ new romantic relationships.
- Same again in potential breakups.
- Moved away from parents for the first time (thank goodness for dorms).
- Moved to a new state for the summer.
- Started an internship at a new company.
- Tried the intramural ultimate frisbee team.
- Learned how to use crutches after frisbee got heated.
- Joined SWE...

Whatever the count, and whatever the *right* number is for you, transitions come into your life demanding attention, and hand delivering you stress.

In Chapter 4 we're going to look at how trusting yourself, being present, thoughtfully prioritizing, and dedicating time to self-care can help you flourish today. We'll review practical tools to thrive right now. We will use transitions (aka our beautifully annoying stress packages) as checkpoints since these are typically when a bit of extra attention can go a very long way.

Understand the Emotional Rollercoaster

Most transitions in life come with a few highs and lows. Starting a new job is an example of a full-on emotional rollercoaster we often do not prepare for adequately. It is the best, and then the worst, and then it's hopefully the best again.

When you decide to make a large professional change, you are excited to get going. You want to meet the team and learn what they're working on, what's going well, and what you can fix with your amazing toolbox of skills you're bringing with you.

And then—*oh shit*.

As with any transition, successfully navigating the time before and after a new job requires a significant dose of patience—especially patience with yourself.

For example, imagine you've just accepted your dream job as a software engineer on a team of analytical geniuses developing the world's most ground-breaking new widget.

1 You are so excited the whole week before your start date. You just want to get going!

2 You didn't manage to sleep at all the night before, but people seem very nice today. The hardest thing for you to learn is where the bathrooms are located.

3 Three days in you are pleased to realize you've joined an awesome team, but there are also a surprising number of acronyms you've never heard before.

4 The second week you get assigned a design task. It's not a super tough one, and hypothetically you should be able to work it quickly, but you don't have access to the server yet. Your emotional high starts to waver...

Welcome to the Emotional Rollercoaster!

Image a simple two axis graph with a single line rising and falling. The x-axis is time; the y-axis is your resilience throughout this transitional period. You are in the rollercoaster car rolling along, maybe in full control, or maybe with your hands over your head screaming.

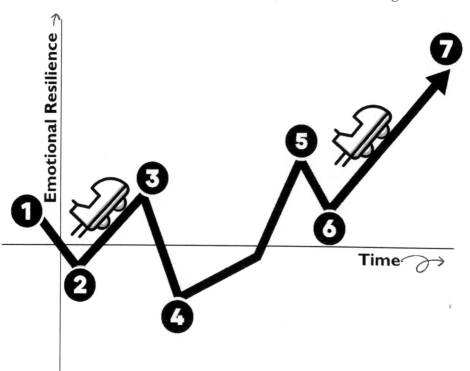

Continuing along this hypothetical new career as a widget designer extraordinaire...

5 You've started completing tasks and feel like you are contributing.

6 There is so much more to learn. Did you make the right choice?

7 You're becoming the go-to for something. People are beginning to trust you and you even made a friend. You've got this!

Every transition is going to be a slightly different ride. Sometimes onboarding will proceed smoothly. Other times you will be adrift, making it all up as you go. But if you watch yourself carefully, themes will begin to emerge in your personal life-changes amusement park.

The tools in Chapter 4 are designed to help you bring your hands and feet back inside the car and enjoy the ride with confidence and intention—*permanecer sentados por favor*.[1]

Good news!

Most companies and teams understand any new employee is an investment. Rarely does someone come out of the gate fully competent to deliver the same way someone with years in the position would. A learning curve is expected, as is some level of on-the-job training.[2]

In theme park terms, this investment can be visualized as a steadily inclining ride with no planned drops, loops, or spirals—much more like a cable car lifting you to the top of an epic mountain.

The very same cable car, which seems so steady and safe, is the culprit for internalized stress throughout the first weeks and months of a large

---

[1] Translation: "Remain seated please" from the Matterhorn, 1992.

[2] For more about the concept of company investment and dividends, see Michael Watkin. *The First 90 Days*. Boston: Harvard Business Review Press, 2003.

transition. You know they expect returns on their investment. Every win might be paired with a growing pressure to add even more value.

While technical skill growth and business learning might be linear, personal experience is not as steady. Add in the impacts of this change on your home life and self-care routine, and it's got the potential to get a bit bumpy.

Not to worry. With awareness of what's to come each day, your transition can be significantly more manageable. Maybe even fun. Knowing your tendencies on these rides can help you prepare and thrive.

Use the space below to reflect on recurring trends you experienced in your past career transitions. What emotions did you feel throughout? At what point did you feel fully transitioned?

Reflection Space: Past Transitions

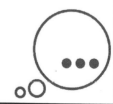

We need change in our life—at least occasionally. If you're courageous enough to buckle up and embark, you will learn so much. You will make connections and build trust. You will become the technical expert for something you love. And then you will know you are crushing it.

Maybe at some point you'll realize you're not learning enough anymore, and you'll want to take another step forward in your career. Then you buckle your seatbelt again as you prepare for your next big transition.

Leverage the Emotional Rollercoaster

When viewed as one big ride, any transition can seem overwhelming. Thankfully though, the emotional rollercoaster tends to roll through a handful of generally independent phases. In each phase expectations change—your own expectations and those of your boss, work colleagues, and home team. The tools available to leverage for success will also shift.

We'll look together at each of the five phases:

Phase 1 - Anticipating Change (aka pre-start)

Phase 2 - Climbing the Learning Curve

Phase 3 - Delivering with Confidence

Phase 4 - Doubting (because unfortunately we all do it)

Phase 5 - Creating Value

Let's look deeper into the tools and strategies that might serve you in each unique phase of your transition, starting before you even start.

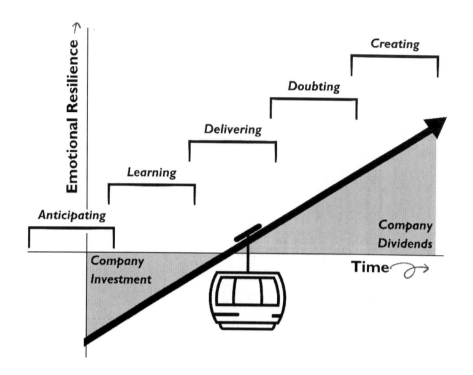

Phase 1 – Anticipate Change

You are excited. This is new. You may also be anxious and possibly annoyed you can't start right now.

Phase 1 typically presents itself both before the start and often into the first week or so as well. It is the time between saying yes to the new opportunity (or maybe hearing you've been tapped to take this on) and the time when you have all the tools in hand to really get started.

This is a fabulous moment to take a deep breath and dedicate some time to planning. It is also an excellent time for a bit of extra self-care. Working parents spend so much of their lives spreading themselves thin. Pausing just for you sounds almost unheard of. It can be just the trick though to setting yourself up for a smooth and positive next adventure.

The Phase 1 checklist offers three actionable steps to do just that.

Transitions Checklist
PHASE I - ANTICIPATING

- [ ] **Negotiate to create and protect a pause.**
- [ ] **Check in on your home operating rhythm.**
- [ ] **Research.**

The first action is to negotiate for you and your time. It's your opportunity to be an advocate for yourself. The days before you start a new job are a rare and beautiful moment of pause. Take care of yourself by creating a few days or weeks of time off to decompress from the last job, do something for you that you've been putting off, and make time to prepare for the next.

If you are going to a new company, negotiate a start date far enough out to take a breather. Consider if you can afford a few weeks of *funemployment* during the switch.[3] Imagine a magic bubble in time where you get to play. The kid's daycare routine is still in place. Your partner is still going to work. And you can do absolutely anything!

If you are staying with the same company, you should still negotiate. You were selected for this new role for a reason. It is highly unlikely they would nix their top candidate because she requested to use a week of her already earned vacation to reset. You can still call it funemployement too, even though you are collecting a paycheck the whole time.

---

[3] Funemployment: Fun meets unemployment. Whether you have limited financial responsibilities or have built a savings buffer, taking a few weeks of self-funded time off during a job transition can be a welcome self-care treat.

Given that over 765 million vacation days went unused in the US in 2022, there's a good chance you have a few PTO hours to spare.[4] This is of course assuming you don't have a kid who just started kindergarten. If you do, you have probably already burned every hour on runny noses. In that case, can you negotiate for more vacation time?

If you're like me, you might also feel a bit of guilt about leaving the last team behind. I find myself wanting to hang on to help them as long as possible. Then I remember, they will be fine.

To create the space we need in our transitions, we need to close out the role—completely. Answering a question here or there is ok. Having any responsibility for deliverables is not. They will learn to swim without you.

Once you've sufficiently padded your work stop and next start, the next action is to check in with your home / life operating rhythm.

How will this new role you're taking impact your current home operating rhythm? It's possible you will very soon be on more calls, commuting farther or at different times. Maybe you will have more days working from home and want to reduce (or increase) the time your family is out of the house.

Consider where you will now need help from others. Do you need to enlist your partner's or community's support? Conversely, are there things you previously needed help with that you want to pick up again?

Now consider how you are going to make time for yourself. Do you need to change which days you attend your favorite yoga class or what night is going to be order-in night? Is anything you love at risk of getting squeezed out of your weekly plan?

If yes, how are you going to protect it?

Rather than jumping into the next chapter at full throttle and with no heading, take a moment to consider how you and your home team can set yourselves up for a smooth transition. Once you have a plan, consider if there's time to do a dry run before the big day.

---

[4] See Anna Baluch. *Average PTO in the US & other PTO statistics (2023)*. Forbes.com/advisor for more staggering stats.

The third action for creating positive momentum while you're anticipating the start of your next adventure is to do your homework. Focus your energy on researching what you don't know yet but think you might wish you knew very soon.

Research can take many forms. Consider internet searches, asking friends in the area, investing in a bit of targeted training, or taking someone out for coffee. Get creative (as long as it's ethical). Is there a movie that everyone in your new field will have watched? Dedicate those 2 hours and have some popcorn.

Subjects can include, but are not limited to, your new role, your team, the company, the industry, lunch options near the office…

Investing a bit of time up front will boost your confidence on Day 1. This might just help ease some of those drops on your upcoming rollercoaster ride.

Moral of the Phase 1 story, enjoy the pause. Use the space available to set yourself up for success, and that includes taking care of *you* a bit more than normal. When you get to work on Day 1 and they don't have your laptop ordered yet, take a deep breath, and continue investing in learning and self-care.

Phase 2 – Climb the Learning Curve

Welcome to the grace period. People want you to succeed and they are here to help you. The length and volume of this grace is highly variable. If you are a new graduate, people will invest heavily in your learning without any notable contributions back for months. If you are an executive taking the helm of a high-profile division, you might get 6 hours.

When I was asked to take a three-month assignment to course correct a challenged team, I knew I had to climb my learning curve fast. I held onto my *Newbie Card* for three days. Then I used what I had learned during my very brief Phase 2 to pivot toward delivering with confidence.

From a hiring manager's perspective, this investment phase is not a surprise. We know staffing a team with skilled individuals takes time. We've already invested time into job postings, interviews, down selects, offers, and negotiations.[5] A bit more time to bring our new team member up to speed not only makes sense, it's also much more time effective than going back to square one with a new posting.

From the newbie card holder's perspective, climbing the learning curve can be exciting and daunting.

Let's look at steps you can take to enhance your emotional resilience during Phase 2.

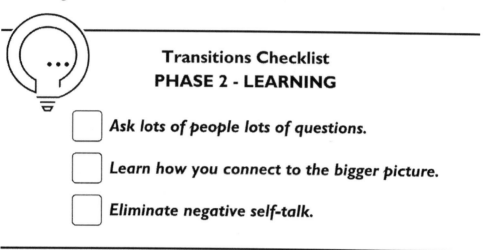

Transitions Checklist
PHASE 2 - LEARNING

☐ *Ask lots of people lots of questions.*

☐ *Learn how you connect to the bigger picture.*

☐ *Eliminate negative self-talk.*

The first action is to grab a notebook and start scribbling down questions as they hit you—in meetings, during training, that weird thing you overheard across the cubical wall. If you are in an acronym heavy industry (and what STEM mom isn't?) collect all of these on a separate page of your notebook.

So much of the learning curve climb is about who, not what. Spend time learning *who* you trust and the *what* will become much easier.

Choose who you would like to connect with more and find logical times to ask them a handful of the questions. I always found spreading out the questions to be highly useful. Simpler questions that need to be asked could be directed to a new peer. Tough questions can be addressed with

---

[5] Reminder: Always negotiate.

potential mentors. Spreading the questions around will help you learn who you naturally connect with.

Also consider that not every question needs to be asked. Apparently young children ask 25 questions an hour at home.[6] We don't want to remind anyone of their four-year-old in the office. Keep your eyes and ears open and many of your questions will answer themselves.

Of course, there is a *what* too. You were hired to do something—be it engineering, pipetting, managing, or basket weaving. As you engage with the responsibilities of your role, your second Phase 2 action is to learn about your role and how it connects into the bigger picture.

Imagine for a moment, an awe-inspiring impressionist pointillism painting stretched from wall to wall in a historic museum. Some renaissance artist painstakingly applied hundreds of thousands of dots on a canvas, all playing together to create a masterpiece of lilies or a riverside picnic.

Thankfully in today's corporate roles, you are unlikely to be responsible for every dot on the canvas. You will be responsible for some though. As you learn the color and location of your dots (bear with me here), wouldn't it be useful to know what it is the team is painting... aka the big picture?!

Ok, enough metaphor.

The point is you can and should learn how to execute and deliver well in your role. But you will also benefit from learning about the bigger picture. Knowing why the pink copy goes to accounting and the fuchsia one goes to purchasing might not help you today, but in the long run it will make you a more valuable employee because you will see past the silo of your individual role to the larger system.

If you feel valuable, you are going to be more emotionally resilient when things get tougher.

The third action is related to self-care... again!

---

[6] See Paul Harris. "What children learn from questioning." ERIC.ed.gov. September 2015.

In this magical grace period, people are giving you space to learn. Be graceful with yourself as well. Striving to learn everything we can as fast as we can often quickly feels discouraging. It's intense, and those little voices of negative self-talk that start to creep in at tough moments can sound so logical.

Personally, while Phase 2 learning is exciting, it is also where I typically experience my first rollercoaster dip. For better or worse, we all have a small gremlin in our psyche who chimes in at highly inconvenient times to tell us we're not going to succeed. Some call this voice imposter syndrome. Shirzad Chamine, who has researched positive mental fitness extensively, calls that negative self-talk our *resident saboteur*.

According to Chamine, our saboteur first shows up when we're children "as our guardians to help us survive the real and imagined threats to our physical and emotional survival." It's when that troublesome instigator hangs around into adulthood that they become negative "invisible inhabitants of our mind."[7]

These little furballs in our brains thrive at creating stress and frustration. Some people are naturally skilled at ignoring their negative self-talk, while others struggle. Fortunately, there are ways we can all manage our resident saboteurs.

The first step is to acknowledge it, but don't feed or water it (especially if it's a gremlin!). Picture the personification of all your doubts—that voice that sneaks up at the wrong moment to poke at your plans.

This little pest might feel like an alien occupying prime real estate inside your very own head without any efforts to pay rent. They don't even do that half-reach-for-the-wallet thing when the check comes.

Let's take some power away from that troublemaker.

It's activity time again. Draw them.

---

[7] Check out the Positive Intelligence website for a quiz on your saboteur. See *How we self sabotage*. 2023. PositiveIntelligence.com/saboteurs.

Art Project
ACKNOWLEDGING
YOUR SABOTEUR

Create a caricature of your personal nay-sayer.
Have fun, add accessories, and give them a name.

Hello!
my name is

Take a minute to reflect on your art project. How did drawing your saboteur change how you plan to engage with them going forward? Do you plan to refer to them by name now? Capture your thoughts in the box below.

Reflection Space: Taking Your Saboteur's Power

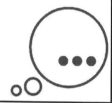

Now that we are on familiar terms, we can take away our nay-sayer's words. Phase 2, Action 3 is to actively cut negative self-talk from your vocabulary. Don't say anything out loud that undercuts your capability, especially not whispered under your breath.

Easy rule of thumb for this one: If you wouldn't say it about another human, why would you say it to yourself?

I found my saboteur was strongest in my early years of parenthood. Talk about a rollercoaster of a transition! I realized at some point that I continuously made quips like *Ah, I'm a bad mom*. I meant them as a joke, but why was I saying it at all?

By eliminating the negative self-talk, even when it was meant as a silly self-deprecating joke, I quieted my saboteur and gave myself space to learn and grow. This is key to setting up for the thrilling third phase, the part where we start getting it done!

Phase 3 – Deliver with Confidence

Phase 3 is a sneaky one. You don't always see it coming. You've been in the job for a bit, you are starting to meet people, and just this morning you realized you understood what some of the people were talking about in the daily stand up. And then it happens…

You're adding value!

It might have been helping someone log into the newest post-processing software. It might have been completing your first big assignment, or a small but challenging task. It might have been as simple as taking a moment to introduce two people who have worked near each other for years but had never realized they both love peppermint tea.

Whatever it is, you made a difference, and it feels good. That rollercoaster is ticking back up. You just might be getting your feet under you, so what should you do now?

Transitions Checklist
PHASE 3 - DELIVERING

☐ **Trust yourself.**

☐ **Practice talking about your accomplishments.**

☐ **Prioritize your work.**

As you build familiarity with your role, allow your confidence to grow too. Practice trusting yourself and allow others to trust you too.

We've already started one excellent way of building self-trust—pull forward your newfound awareness of your saboteur and continue noticing when your thoughts and words are harmful. Checking in often will build a practice of awareness that has the potential to grow into control. And who doesn't think mind control is cool?

Other ways to practice trust include building up your informal network of support, focusing your time on people who build you up.

We don't have time for those who tear others down.

You can also set goals and then reward yourself when you achieve them.

Treat yo' self! **Donna & Tom**

aka Retta & Aziz Ansari

The goals could be from your Chapter 3 maps, or detailed actions aligned to the day job. Whatever the task, figure out how you like to be recognized and then treat yourself.[8]

The second action is to share your accomplishments with others. It is not bragging. It's facts and data. Communication regarding the value you create is data they need to support your tasking and development. It also makes their life easier they are responsible for providing you with feedback on your performance.

Women in the workforce systematically undersell their abilities. Research continuously highlights our persistent modesty. One study showed we undersell our achievements by a whopping 33% as compared to our male counterpart.[9] Another measured that we are 20% better at upselling our friends' abilities than our own.[10]

---

[8] Shout out to the TV series "Parks and Recreation" on NBC for celebrating characters who celebrate themselves.

[9] See National Bureau of Economic Research (NBER). "Women persistently sell themselves short of same-skill men." *NBER, The Digest.* December 2019.

[10] See Carol Schmidt. "Bragging rights: MSU study shows that interventions help women's reluctance to discuss accomplishments." *Montana State University.* January 10, 2014.

This is NOT because we don't value our worth. If you are reading this book, you are looking to grow and develop your best career and life. That is not the mindset of someone who does not know they are capable.

Instead, the studies highlight only that we find ourselves unconsciously, and sometimes consciously, beholden to societal biases. We are expected to be modest and appreciative.

The effects of these social norms mean we experience discomfort when we try to self-promote.

For example, when I describe myself to others, I am a mom and engineer with 16 years of aerospace experience. This is accurate, honest, and not very flashy. I don't want anyone to think I'm bragging or trying to prove I'm better than them. But when my sister wrote an essay about our family in college, she boldly described me as "a blonde bombshell rocket scientist."

Doh! It's embarrassing to even copy that sentence here. It had to be done though, because it is proof that our friends and sisters are often more complimentary about us than we are willing to be about ourselves.

Since I shared my cringe story, I get to make you do the same. Check out the pop quiz on the next page to test the depth of your self-promotion bias.

Pop Quiz
SELF-PROMOTION
SOMATIC MARKERS

Step 1: *Circle all the somatic markers that you experience when considering the following action.*

> **Action:**
> **Write a post for social media that celebrates just how amazing you are.**

Somatic Markers

Brow furrowed	Shoulders tight	Sweating
Eye twitching	Arms crossed	Queasy
Leaning away	Leaning in	Stomach knotted
Fists tight	*Write in:* _____	

Results

If (Markers = 0) ⟶ You have a rare gift. Consider how you can coach others to share their accomplishments more comfortably.

If (Markers > 0) ⟶ You are in good company. Recognize without judgement and keep moving forward.

Step 2: *Actually write and post that positive message about your skills and accomplishments.*

Would it help to think of this task as self-advocacy rather than self-promotion?

Fortunately, there is hope! We can fight this currently systemic gender promotion gap. We can make progress through practice and a few clever interventions. According to Harvard's professional development team, women can practice "healthy self-promotion" by keeping a few tips and tricks in mind.[11]

Use "I" statements.

Cut "we" from your self-promotion vocabulary. It's a subtle shift that your audience might not even catch, but it's huge in conveying your specific value. You can also say how fantastic Suli was, but when you're talking about yourself, make sure they know it's you who did the work.

Be visible.

Where you sit does matter. You belong there, take up space like you know it. Similarly, stand in the circle at daily standups if able. And if anyone in your group is not able, maybe encourage the whole team to sit.

Request high visibility work.

Make it hard for others to not see how well you are doing. Volunteer for the hard stuff. Request stretch tasks, and then let your work speak for itself.

Skip the Nonpromotable Tasks (aka NPTs).

NPTs are all those small tasks that should be done by someone but hold no developmental value. Research shared in *The No Club* found women are much more likely to take on NPTs, and we are often saying we'd be "happy to" as we do. But why? Next time you're asked to drop your high-value work to help with the seating chart replan, or to update the website, or nurse a team member's experiment because he's

---

[11] See Pamela Reynolds. "Women don't self-promote, but maybe they should." *Professional Development, Harvard Division of Continuing Education.* July 11, 2022.

working on another project... stop saying yes. Set boundaries and join the *No Club*.[12]

Find advocates.

Hopefully you already have someone in your corner cheering for you. Whether it's your boss, mentor, coffee buddy, or team co-lead, let them know you could use some support. Men and women can help share stories of your contributions to the powers that be. Most allies are looking for ways to help—make it easy for them by asking!

Healthy self-advocacy is the act of honestly sharing what you did that was exceptional without coming across like you are trying to undercut others or overtly get ahead.

When it comes to writing about our amazingness, something that is often crucial for landing the next interview or promotion, we need to close that 20-33% gap.

Consider establishing a practice of celebrating the awesome work your friends are doing. Observe the language choices you make for them. Once you get used to recognizing others, apply similar diction and emotive articulation to your own accomplishments.

Perhaps you can write your next bio, resume, or cover letter from the perspective of your best friend. When done, read it, smile, and don't be tempted to change or undercut the content. [13]

You can even go one step farther and reread your final document imaging it is written for a competent male peer. If you notice anything odd or undersold for him, enhance the word choice for you. This strategy comes from Kristen Pressner's TEDx talk where she encourages everyone to "flip it to test it." If the reverse seems weird, there's probably

[12] See Linda Babcock, Brenda Peyser, Lise Vesterlund, and Laurie Weingart. *The No Club: Putting a Stop to Women's Dead-End Work.* New York: Simon & Schuster, 2022.
[13] See Kuheli Dutt, Danielle L Pfaff, Joseph S Dillard, and Caryn J Block. "Gender differences in recommendation letters for postdoctoral fellowships in geoscience." *Nature Geoscience.* October 3, 2016.

some bias to go back and tackle. Since we all have unconscious biases, this is a valuable tool for us all to apply. [14]

Now that you and your advocates are joyfully singing your praises and earning all the recognition you deserve (right?), what is it that you should be working on anyway?

The third action for Phase 3 of this transition is to prioritize well and figure out what you can delegate.

Prioritization is fundamental to a successful day-to-day.

Sometimes work will be clearly prioritized for you. Do A, then B, then C. As you climb the ranks the order and value of each task gets murkier. Do you need to review the performance report first, have that coaching discussion, or approve the purchase orders? Fewer people are telling you what to do and autonomy becomes the expectation.

Checking Advocacy Bias

As leaders we can all be more aware of how unconscious bias impacts the gender gap.

Women learn through hard knocks that singing their praises is risky and then adjust accordingly. But it's not just a self-advocacy issue.

A Columbia University team studied 1,224 letters of recommendation written by men and women proponents. They found women candidates are half as likely to receive excellent letters compared to their male peers. Only half!

Next time you are asked to write anything for a woman, please double check your biases. Reread the entire letter as if it were meant to recommend a man. What do you need to change? Make the changes before you submit.

---

[14] For more, including Kristen Pressner's "flip it to test it" strategy, watch *TEDxBasel: Are you biased? I am.* August 30, 2016.

When I was first entering the world of management, I thought I loved autonomy—finally, no one was telling me what to do! But alas, just because no one told me what to do did not mean that I was not acutely aware I had A LOT to do.

A month into my new role (yay, Phase 3) we threw a birthday party for my littlest one. Balloons were everywhere.

Like any good party, kids bashed those balloons up, down, over, sideways, into the wall, and off their friends' heads. The logic of the activity, if any logic can be found with three-year-olds, was to keep the balloons off the floor as much as possible.

Back in the office on Monday, staring at my list of tasks, all I could see was balloons... balloons I had to keep off the floor.

Unlike at the party where the game (aka self-organized pandemonium) held little consequence, my tasks could have serious ramifications if they dropped. And I did not have the benefit of cake.

After analysis, I realized some tasks were simple and required little attention—it was like they were helium filled balloons. A light bump would allow me to leave them unattended for long stretches of time. Things like completing my annual training, cleaning my inbox, and attending quarterly all-hands meetings required little effort or forethought.

Other balloons felt like they were filled with lead. I would lift them up and they would fall back hard. These showed up as product quality concerns, low performers actively degrading team culture, or a livid customer who was demanding a contract rewrite. These needed to be addressed quickly and then removed from the party entirely.

Most balloons were in the middle. Performance metrics needed constant touches but were rarely heavy. Employee salary reviews were heavy but rarely touched.

This mental model has helped me prioritize my workload for years now. Whether you connect to the balloon imagery or not, the fundamentals remain—some tasks have high impact. They require a lot of attention and a high touch rate. Some tasks do not.

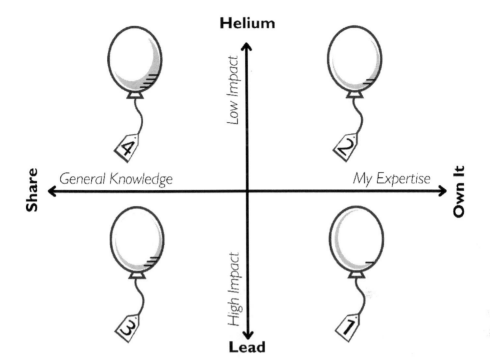

At the same time, some small and large issues don't require one specific person to solve them. We should consider delegating these balloons to the right person.

By laying out the impact of each task versus the skills required, we can prioritize our work efficiently.

For the x-axis, ask yourself if you are the right person to do this work. Are you the only person who can? Odds are someone else can help or it might be time to start developing your delegate.

For the y-axis, consider if the issue needs to be addressed immediately. What is the impact on the team or business if it isn't addressed today. Tasks that require action go toward the bottom of the grid. Let other tasks float up to the top.

Remember, neither axis is binary, use it as a sliding scale to place your many tasks. We'll look at each quadrant individually to identify specific actions we can take for each type of balloon we encounter.

Priority 1 Action: Focus and Finish

In the first quadrant we have issues that are high impact, and you are uniquely skilled or empowered to address them. These are your bread and butter. They will take up a large portion of most days.

They are also the high visibility tasks we mentioned as part of your self-promotion plan. Take these challenges on and close them out. This is why you are here crushing it.

It is easy to get hyper focused on Priority 1 balloons. They are flashy and fun. These are the problems you went to school for or stepped into management to take on at full throttle!

Just be careful you don't forget the rest of your responsibilities. Take a quick pause each morning to check in on your other balloons. If any of them are losing altitude, you might need to plan some dedicated time soon, lest they become lead weights as well.

Priority 2 Action: Plan Check Points

You are the right person for these tasks, and for good reason. They are not as critical, but they're yours. As a leader this could be any task that required you to access HR records or salary information. As a technical expert, you might need to conduct a technical review of your mentee's paper that's due at the end of the quarter. If you are an individual contributor, you might have a deep stack of specialized tasks, and certain balloons naturally float easier.

Sometimes we get lost in the second quadrant because it feels good to get stuff accomplished, and this work is far less stressful than Priority 1 tasks.

Plan how you will keep Priority 2 tasks moving. If you don't have a lot of Priority 1, that should be simple. If you are a leader who's always fighting fires, check in at the start of the week to assess the scale of your near term just-need-to-get-it-done tasks. Write a checklist for the week. Then block out specific time and get it done.

A highlight of my management career was when a senior engineer walked into my office and thanked me for taking care of the small stuff quickly. I had approved a software request that had just hit my inbox. By remembering there are some unglamorous tasks only I can do, I cleared the way for him to do the tasks that only he can do. Eight years later the same now-former employee sent me a second note of gratitude for consistently completing the small stuff quickly.

Don't forget Priority 2 work. It matters—most often to the people we are here to support.

Priority 3 Action: Coach Someone

Who can benefit from a tougher assignment or wants to develop in this area? Priority 3 tasks are important, they need a lot of touches, but they don't need you.

These tasks are your opportunity to practice your coaching skills. Delegate the tasks by establishing requirements, clearly articulating expectations, and setting intermediate checkpoints. While you will need to keep an eye on these efforts, you won't need to be the one doing the work.

According to Deloitte's 2023 Women@Work research, 51% of women report higher stress levels than the previous year. More than a quarter of us feel burnt out. Imagine if we could let go of even a sliver of what we're doing and at the exact same time empower and support another person's growth.

How?

Make a list of all your tasks. Include the big rocks down to the grains of sand (because if you've ever been to a beach, you've seen that those can add up too!). Consider how each task floats onto this grid. For any that drift to the third quadrant, consider who would benefit from taking it on.

While you might not see it as a big task, the new hire next to you might be craving a chance to demonstrate their ability to deliver consistently.

Priority 4 Action: Let it Float Away

Tasks in the fourth quadrant have a low impact on the team and business. They do not require regular attention or any unique skills. So why are we working on them at all? Write these down on a separate list and let them go.

Priority 4 tasks can grab your attention and pull you in. But when all is said and done, you'll hit "save to desktop," and then... nothing.

I have lost full days revising documents for meetings that will never be scheduled. I lost half a week strategizing how we could implement a second shift of engineers for a team I didn't manage, when the real problem was the organization was understaffed and not communicating.

Call them red-herrings, shiny object, pet projects, anything. Just don't call them yours.

If you're ready to practice, use the following grid to sort your to-do list. Consider how important each item is, how often it needs attention, and if you are truly the right person to do that work. Include as much or as little detail as you need to effectively categorize your workload into the four quadrants.

Once sorted, the second step is to determine what actions you can take with this new awareness. Use your new plan to prioritize and delegate this week.

Prioritization
SORTING OUT BALLOONS

Step 1: Capture all current tasks on the grid below.
Critically consider each task and if you need to be the person working it.

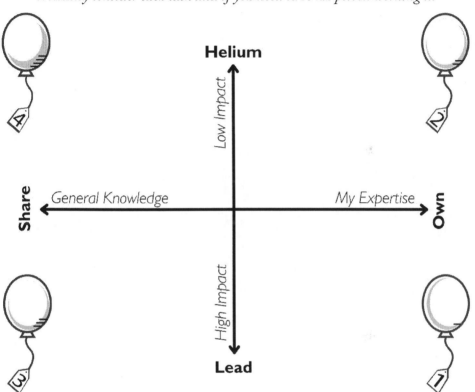

Step 2: Build this week's plan based on grid placement.

 **Let go:**

Dedicate time for:

 **Delegate:**

Focus on:

It might be worth stopping by elmmcoaching.com for more copies of this worksheet. Maybe this could become part of your weekly routine!

With Phase 3 well in hand, you are now feeling strong and delivering with confidence. You know the work that's coming your way and how to celebrate when you crush it. You are set up for success, even if that emotional rollercoaster takes a dip one more time… which it might.

Phase 4 – Manage Doubt

So… *Mom Guilt* is real, and it can be a very strong emotion. It is a feeling you can't seem to shake. What if the choices I'm making today are not helping my kids? Or even worse, what if I'm irreversibly messing them up?!

Guilt itself is a social emotion that is learned through life. Mom guilt (or caregiver guilt, self-doubt…) is a special sub-species of social emotional learning that connects everything we do to these little humans we've created and really want to do right by. It makes us doubt our choices time after time, leaving us exhausted.

I am not proposing here that these feelings are unique to STEM moms—however as an engineer, leader, and mom myself I find I am often acutely aware that my team of peers who can empathize with me on a rough day is limited.

Phase 4 of our adventure is the time to think about tricks and tools to manage doubt and guilt. This is the time when our rollercoaster ride is trying its best to get a scream out of us, and we don't have to let it.

Transitions Checklist
PHASE 4 - DOUBTING

- [ ] *Find your village (and name it).*

- [ ] *Be present where you are present.*

- [ ] *Set boundaries.*

The first action is to find a support system. The benefits of feeling truly supported are invaluable. We looked at the power of investing in a network back in Chapter 3 when we considered the expanded technical and leadership growth grid. In Chapter 5 we will go deep into building mentoring partnerships. So here in Chapter 4, Phase 4, we'll focus on your village.

Having a village of supporters and mentors when the going gets tough makes the tough feel manageable. They don't need to be people on your new work team or even in your company. If you just did a big career jump, they likely won't be.

Who are your people?

Who do you trust to bounce thoughts and ideas off?

Having people in your corner is powerful. I have learned there's even more power in naming your team(s). Even with seemingly casual friend groups, by naming ourselves we create a profound sense of belonging and inclusion.

The women I connected with in prenatal yoga became my "yoga mommas" when we started meeting for tea regularly post-partum.

Twelve years later we still go on family vacations together and meet for highchair happy hours (HCHH).[15]

The people I ride bikes with are called Soft Like Kitten. It's a ridiculous team name that adds no clarity to who we are or what we do, but it reminds us we have people to call when we don't want to ride in the rain alone.

 Be present where you are present.

At work I am part of the Class of 2016 Emerging Leaders Development Program (aka ELDP, because STEM loves acronyms). Without our name we would just be people who took some leadership classes together and attended the same tours. By adding a name, we have an identity and a shared unspoken commitment to support each other.

Wherever and whomever your village may be, play with the idea of adding a name. It could be as simple as naming your text group or as elaborate as printing t-shirts. Most importantly, make sure you're building a village of people you can trust and then call them when you catch yourself starting to doubt.

The second action to manage mom guilt is to practice being present right where you are right now.

Being present where you're present is the practice of reminding yourself that the choices you have made led you to the activity you are participating in right now. Since you are a very smart person and probably quite analytical at times, it is highly unlikely you made all those decisions lightly. Therefore, odds are you are exactly where you are

---

[15] Simple Life Hack: Highchair happy hour (HCHH) is a terrific way to build community. The yoga mommas and our partners have kept this acronym alive long past when the youngest in the group switched to a regular seat at the table.

supposed to be right now. Based on that logic, give yourself permission to fully engage where you are.

It was hard to drop my infant off at daycare with four fresh bottles and two changes of clothes. But then I would get to work and remind myself we had picked the best daycare. I was at work because I chose to be a working parent. I loved my job. Plus I wanted my son to grow up in a world where moms design airplanes.

Reminding myself of this allowed me to focus the next eight hours on meetings, hallway conversations, code de-bugging, and at least two cups of coffee with absolutely no one around me crying to be picked up. I was present.

Then I could pick up my son and give him my full attention.

It's not foolproof, but by being present where you're present you are offering the gift of your attention to the people you are with.

A few tricks for practicing presence:

- Take your hands off your keyboard and phone when someone is talking to you. Bonus points if you can bring yourself to turn your feet to face them. It's harder than it sounds.
- Trust that you have a sound childcare plan so you can work a full day fully focused on your job. If you can't, make a change.
- Leave work behind when you choose to leave at the end of the day. Can you leave your laptop at the office? Do you really need your work phone?
- If you work from home, develop an end-of-work routine to shut down one activity and give your brain space to switch to the next. Consider a walk around a block, a shower, or a change of clothes. Maybe it's 10 minutes with an audiobook or your favorite pre-pandemic radio station.

Possibly the hardest form of presence to commit to is when you try to create space just for yourself. As caregivers and partners people are always looking forward to engaging. As valued team members and leaders others need your input all the time. When you *do* need alone time, it is hard to protect your space. This is where boundaries come into play!

Action 3 is setting clear and maintainable boundaries.

When my sister needed three hours of uninterrupted space to build a presentation for her next board meeting, she put a post-it on her office door. It read...

Honest and clear. She communicated what her current priority was and set expectations for what she considered to be an acceptable interruption. As you can see, it was a high threshold. In this case no one interrupted her, and the board meeting went great!

Where would you like to establish and maintain boundaries to improve your own state of mind during the day? Would articulating when you will be arriving and leaving work each day help others know when they can find you and when they should hold their questions?

Perhaps a daily plan that's actually written down could help align you and your partner on who needs to get what done. That way, when you choose to stay late for that recurring Tuesday evening meeting, you know someone else knows they are on point for pick-up.

If your office has asked you to come back into the office, consider what boundaries and accommodations you need to be successful at work and home. This counts as a transition, even if you're on the same team doing the same tasks. Prepare for a round of mom guilt and plan boundaries to support you.

Boundaries can be as simple as shutting the door when you need a moment to exhale. Or if you know a closed door is not a clear enough clue for your toddler, maybe you want to establish that your personal time is out of the house.

As a manager, I always took time to articulate with new teams the best ways to communicate with me. I would share that if I were listed in the CC line of an email, I would assume it was sent for reference only and they should not expect a reply. Conversely, if the email was only sent to me, I established an expectation that I would reply within 24 hours. Outlook color coding helped me meet that goal many times!

Quick check in. With all this new clarity on boundaries, does your family operating rhythm need to be updated? If the current plan doesn't allow

Advocating for Personal Agency

To build high performing teams, we must cultivate a culture of engagement. Engaged employees are more productive, and more productive employees raise the bottom line.

McKinsey & Company's "Women in the Workplace 2022" report highlights that to engage, you must offer choice.

Work arrangements are an easy and empowering way to offer choice. According to the workplace report, when you offer your team the power to choose virtual, hybrid, or in person, your employees will be "less burned out, happier in their jobs, and much less likely to consider leaving their companies."

Are you offering your team agency?

you to leave work behind, could you add an hour of childcare to create a mental buffer?

Or maybe you see a glaring gap in self-care and need to make a change?

Embrace your iterative design skills and treat Phase 4 as an empowerment checkpoint. You started this transition with a well thought out plan, but since then you have learned a lot. What needs to shift?

Have the conversations you need to have with your home team and consider what needs to be discussed at work as well.

Remember, while you might be struggling a bit at this moment, you are also starting to make solid contributions at work. Your new team has been investing in you for weeks or months at this point. You are now an asset they know they need to keep.

If something needs to change, plan your logical rationale, do a quick sanity check with a mentor, and then go ask for it.

Phase 5 – Create Value

You've made it through this transition!

You navigated pre-start anticipation, climbing the learning curve, starting to deliver with confidence, and a bit of doubt that cropped up along the way. Learning will continue, doubt might occasionally appear, but for the most part you are now on solid footing moving forward. You are establishing yourself as a key team member and leader. This is the fun part.

When you reach the point of being fully transitioned, you might not even notice it. The job is still challenging, but you are gaining a suite of knowledge and resources to tackle those challenges. There will still be ups and downs on this ride, but with the tools covered in Phases 1-4 you are armed and ready to take them on.

So now what?

Transitions Checklist
PHASE 5 - CREATING

☐ *First, do your day job well.*

☐ *Invest in yourself.*

☐ *Dare to say no.*

Phase 5's actions are highly intertwined. With this abundance of opportunity, remember to keep doing your day job really well. When you have bandwidth, consider what more you want to take on to help you thrive. Say no to the rest.

If you keep your eyes open, an abundance of opportunity surrounds you in this world. Many companies invest in technical, affinity, and social groups. There are charities to support, boards to join, schools to volunteer at, and sports to play.

In my first three months as a professional the opportunities to engage seemed limitless. I was invited to be a founding member of a new early career development program. I was told I should join SWE. My boss was looking for a volunteer to run a recycling program for the building. I was invited to join two company volleyball teams, a softball team (which you might have guessed I declined), and an alpine mountaineering club that I was petrified of.

I could have totally overwhelmed myself and potentially failed entirely at the job I was specifically hired to do. Fortunately, I was paired with a strong mentor who reminded me, "first, do your day job really well." They advised me that even though each opportunity would offer personal and professional growth, they couldn't take me anywhere if I didn't also add value in my assigned job.

It was a well-timed reminder. I picked this job because I wanted to design airplanes. This was a job I wanted to keep!

As Phase 5 progresses, seek out the amazing opportunities that will help you grow and find fulfilment. The best thing you can do for yourself is to say an emphatic *yes* to what excites you, and don't feel pressured to take on the rest because you feel others think you should. *Should* is dangerous. You don't need *should*.

A few things to consider when people are requesting your time:

- Am I excited to do this?
- What will I learn?
- Will this give me energy or take my energy?
- Is the request aligned to my goals and values?

If you don't find yourself answering in the affirmative to most of these questions, you might want to politely decline. Being willing to say no when appropriate will empower you to keep moving forward. You will own your time and will have the ability to invest it as you see fit.

Understand Your Theme Park

After weeks and months of preparation, nerves, learning opportunities, and wins, this rollercoaster is ready to come to an end. As a core contributor now, you have new skills and knowledge. You are investing in others and confident you are spending your time on what matters most.

Every transition is slightly different. After a few you can step back and observe recurring themes. Where do you flourish and where do you struggle? Do you need to make more space for yourself at the beginning of your job changes, or plan for your parents to take the kids for a week one month post start?

What are your somatic markers in each phase? They might soften as you get more comfortable with big transitions or become more pronounced as you add more responsibilities at home.

The more you observe the better you can prepare for next time.

And the best thing is there will be a next time. In any job, when you find you are no longer learning, consider if it's time to get on the next ride. By keeping an eye on your rollercoaster, you will set yourself up for success again.

As you succeed, there is only one more important consideration to cover... how might we build a larger community of support for mothers in STEM?

CHAPTER 5

GROW DIVERSITY IN STEM

L et's look around. If you are in a STEM workspace today, odds are only 1 in 5 people attending your next meeting will be women. If you are a woman, statistically you won't see any other women in your next working group.[1] According to Zippia's *25 Women in Leadership Statistics 2023* report, there's only a 1 in 3 chance your next conversation with a senior leader in any industry will be with a woman. And if you work for a Fortune 500 company you have a 10.4% chance of working for a female CEO.[2]

The SWE conference panel I spoke at in 2021 highlighted for me how many people in under-represented demographics in STEM fields have made it to where we are through gritted teeth and tenacity.

Some have had role models and mentors, some have not.

---

[1] See NCES. *Table 318.30.*

[2] As of June 2023, only 52 (10.4%) of the Fortune 500 CEOs identify female. Only 4 (0.8%) of the same 500 CEOs identify publicly as LGBTQ+. With 50.4% women and 3.8% identifying LGBT in the general population (williamsinstitute.law.ucla.edu), both demographics are significantly underrepresented at the top. For more, see Jim Probasco. "Four openly LGBTQ+ Fortune 500 CEOs and their impact on corporate inclusion." *Investopedia.* February 19, 2023.

Imagine with me what the face of STEM could look like tomorrow if each one of us took the time to turn around and lift as many people as we could.

This lift doesn't need to be arduous. It can be as easy as showing up as yourself. This bravery can create a safe space for others to do the same. Share your stories. Invest some time and energy in meaningful mentoring partnerships.

There are a million tiny moments waiting to be created. Each one is a spark that can inspire a girl, woman, mother, or LGBTQIA+ person to continue with STEM.

Share Your Truth

In 2010 I was petrified to tell my boss I was pregnant. I wasn't scared of retaliation; I had a good boss who I trusted. I was scared because it would be the first time in my career I fully acknowledged I was a woman.

Sounds silly, I know. I'm obviously not a man. This revelation wasn't going to shock anyone. But in a world where I was spending significant energy every single day to *be one of the guys*, this struck me as a huge moment.

Up to that point in my career I had never known another pregnant engineer. I had only heard of one. I was given her desktop computer when I started because she had "been gone a long time."

Apparently, Dr. Anna Fisher, one of the first women selected as a NASA astronaut, went through a similar thought process three decades before me. It was a different time, and unfortunately, she did not have the benefit of trusting her leadership would support her. She knew there was a high chance she would be removed from the training program and mission schedule. Dr. Fisher decided not to tell NASA she was pregnant until she "absolutely had to." In the Netflix show *Like a Mother*, Anna explains that she wanted to "minimize the time that anybody thought [she] was different." I get it Dr. Fisher—thank you for sharing![3]

When I plucked up the courage and told my boss, he was excited and supportive. Even so, I felt like an outsider when he told me I was his

---

[3] Watch *Like a Mother* | *Episode 3: Astronaut*. Produced by Netflix Family. (2021).

first ever pregnant employee. He had been managing for 20 years, and I was the first.

Imagine how much simpler my experience might have been if I had even one shared story to connect to. I would have loved just one person to reassure me I was not doing something audacious.

It took ten more months to realize there were other people in STEM like me. In the office Mother's Room—there was only one in the building—I met six other new moms.

Since we all wanted to pump around the same time, we opted to share the room. In doing so, we created a safe space to share our stories as well. Every new mother was a wonderful new connection. Imagine if I had met them when I was pregnant, or even before. [4]

I heard funny anecdotes, personal struggles, family successes. We were safely hidden away behind a locked door and free to be our whole selves.

I have had twelve years of learning and growing since that first *guess what, I'm a girl!* conversation with my boss. I have built confidence and moved into expanded leadership roles. While I cherish that time in the Mother's Room, I have realized that a couple of couches behind a locked door is not enough. My whole self deserves to be in the open.

Bolstered by my growing skills, network, and credibility, I have explored how to be more me every day. I am motivated by the theory that if as a leader I can be fully me, that might just create space for people earlier in their careers and outside the majority to do the same.

Actions toward this goal are often simple.

Communicate via your calendar.

Mark your family time commitments on your calendar for everyone at work to see. Consider creating meeting notices for each day that you are responsible for morning drop off or

---

[4] "Mother's Room" was the name of the lactation space in my office. I recognize this term is quickly becoming outdated. If you have input on the name of this space at your workplace, please consider using "Lactation Room" to support non-binary parents. If you get to design the space, make sure there is a sink and a fridge.

afternoon pickup. Make the notices transparent, *School Drop Off, 7:30 - 7:50*. If people try to schedule something over that, politely inform them that time is not available.[5]

Use positive word choice.

Diction matters. When tempted to say, *I'm sorry, I have to take my child to a…* instead switch to a confident clear statement with articulated boundaries. *I can work on this until 3:15. Then I will be leaving to get my son to his appointment.* No apologies necessary. Skip the "have to." You are making a choice. Own it.

Use conversation starters.

Add a few pictures of your people to your desk to share your priorities with those interested in knowing. A good picture offers a welcome invitation for conversation to anyone who wants to approach you but doesn't know how to break the ice.

Introduce more of you.

Create an introduction slide when you join a team. Include your name, a bit about your career and education, and what you want others to know about your life (family, where you're from, where you've travelled, hobbies, etc.). Keep it to one page and mainly pictures if possible. Leaders, add a second page about your communication style—how do you want people to connect with you and when you will and won't be available.

Allies, you can do this too! By sharing more about your family and personal priorities you normalize the practice for everyone. I loved when my Chief Engineer stood up and said, "Hi, my name is Dan, and my top priority is spending more time with my grandchildren."

It was simple for him and encouraging for me!

---

[5] There will always be that one meeting that can't be moved and you must adjust. Use your judgment to know when that is and when to hold firm.

Other ideas for how to go big on sharing your story:

- Host a lunchtime roundtable where you answer any question the attendees throw at you candidly. Create a safe space by working with an affiliate group to develop the invite list.
- Start a peer mentoring happy hour or coffee group. Give the group a name!
- Connect with a non-profit that is elevating voices like yours.[6]
- Write a book. Connect with me via cassie@elmmcoaching.com if you want to learn more about how my writing journey is going. Hopefully I can share some tips!

Whatever method excites you, the more you can share your authentic self, the more others will feel empowered to do the same.

Let's take a moment to pause and reflect once again. Use the following space to capture any small or big shifts in your thinking regarding how you want to show up in the workplace and the broader STEM community.

Reflection Space: Share Your Journey

---

[6] Check out the non-profit Mothers in Science. Each month they share a personal story of a STEM mom who is making it work day by day. MothersInScience.com/Journeys.

Embrace "Hard is Hard"

Creating an environment where everyone is authentic and open means you are no longer living on that little one-palm-tree island. You start knowing people who are going through what you are going through. Yay!

But alas, with every win comes a new challenge. You may find you start looking around at your new companions and notice you're not all actually exactly precisely going through the same thing. Please don't let that realization deter you.

One of my most supportive mentors is a senior aerospace executive with two grown boys. As she grew through the ranks, she and her working spouse balanced career progression, baseball teams, business trips, and family vacations. From our very first conversation I was so excited to learn from her!

After a few meetings we got into the details—how had she managed it all?

One of her many brilliant tactics was to enlist her own mother. When business trips were required, she would often bring a son or two and her mom along. The hotel was covered by work, so she just had to fund the flights and some meals—an investment she was willing to make to support her career growth without sacrificing time with family.

It worked for her, but it deflated me. At that time my mom was 1,200 miles away kicking butt operating her own small business. Was my hard harder than my mentor's?

Jumping forward five years, when the pandemic shut it all down, I worked with a strong and dynamic program manager who had two kids the same age as my kids. Her kids were home; my kids were home. We were the same!

Then I learned she and her husband had chosen to start homeschooling well before the pandemic. Her husband's job allowed him to be nearly fully available for the kids on weekdays. As far as I could tell, the only transition that her family faced in early 2020 was their mother's new work-from-home routine. For the most part she was able to use the back bedroom for calls with minimal interruptions. Was her hard less hard than mine?

The more STEM moms and leaders I have met, and the more shared stories I've heard, I've come to this conclusion—nope!

My hard is NOT harder. Hard is just hard.[7]

It in no way served my well-being to compare my situation to others. It is much more valuable to listen to each person's journey and learn how they have navigated their own situation. Many of their creative problem-solving skills have sparked other ideas for me.

More often, I've heard a portion of a solution I can iterate on.

I learned from my mentor with the travelling support team that there is no one way to approach business travel. After many permutations I have refined my own version of business travel to work for me and my family. It includes a lot of mid-morning outbound flights so I can cover one more school drop off and late evening return flights so I can host one last happy hour.[8]

I learned from my new program manager how to set clearer boundaries during working hours. She knew when to close the door and when to let her kids do their homework next to her. While I didn't move my desk into the back bedroom, I did relocate from the kitchen table to my very own makeshift desk in the living room. It's a tiny victory, but I'll take it.

Hard is hard.

Ash Beckham

Coming Out of Your Closet

I have taken these learnings, and learnings from so many other accomplished and inspiring women, to design my version of a winning

---

[7] Ash Beckham uses humor and science to articulate why hard conversations are so hard. Watch "Coming out of your closet." *TEDx Talks*. October 16, 2013.

[8] Simple Life Hack: I also always bring a folding yoga mat and lay it on the floor as soon as a get to the hotel. The visual queue occasionally is enough to remind me to do a bit of self-care.

strategy. Our situations will never be exactly the same, but we can support each other and learn from each other.

And on the very rare occasion you don't pick up a nugget of new wisdom, you've still created room for another person to share their story. Enjoy the connection for the connection. Who knows, the nugget of wisdom might still be coming.

Choose to Mentor

A positive inflection point in my life occurred when I headed to the restroom at a fancy restaurant. Kristin, the division chief engineer and host of the evening, had a similar idea.

Kristin and I talked on the way to the front of the restaurant. Turns out she was also a mom. She and I both had two boys. She was easy to talk to and interested to learn more about me. In less than two minutes I felt a connection and courageously asked her if I could put a 30-minute meeting on her calendar. She said "Yes!"

This meet cute sparked a lasting partnership. For years we met monthly to discuss career, family, balance, opportunity, and technical issues. She would invite me to have dinner with her executive team when she travelled to Seattle. When I was traveling in the Midwest, I would add a day to shadow her and gain new perspective.

One time I ran into Kristin unexpectedly at the Black Engineer of the Year Awards (BEYA) conference in Washington, DC. She gave me a whole-hearted hug right there in the lobby. I felt so welcomed and supported.

As a mentor, Kristin invested her own time in me. We did start in the same organization, but her promotions quickly moved her to another division. She could have dropped me, but she didn't.

Her gracious investment in another helped me in innumerable ways. I had a front row seat to observe a real-life STEM mom and ELMM in action. I gained confidence in my own leadership skills. She offered a sounding board for very difficult issues. And I had someone I trusted when things got hard.

I am very fortunate to have found Kristin at a random business dinner. She is one of a handful of mentors I am incredibly thankful for. Each partnership was a bit awkward to get started. Each connection took courage on my side to ask for support—and graciousness on their side to say yes.

Mentoring is an act of servant leadership. Dedicating specific time to listen to and support others is not easy. We have demanding day jobs, deadlines, personal time commitments, and countless distractions—why add one more thing?

Thankfully, mentors do it anyway. It's probably partly because they see the long-lasting business value in supporting others. Dollars and sense logic does support mentoring.

A recent PNAS study showed that women pursing engineering majors had a significantly higher retention rate in the program after one year when paired with another woman in engineering. [9]

In fact, in the 158-student sample set, women paired with other women were retained in the program at the end of the year. That's zero departures versus the program average attrition of +15%.

Retaining team members will save recruiting and onboarding costs, increase stability, grow productivity, etc. etc. I believe most also choose to mentor because they are just good people.

And then comes the magic…

Once you've overcome the hurdle of fear that you have nothing to offer a mentee, and past the barrier of finding a willing mentee, you will start to realize the bonus value of mentoring. You get to learn as well!

I love that in any mentoring relationships I get to learn. Whether I'm a mentor or mentee doesn't seem to matter. As a mentee, you get to ask questions in a safe space and hopefully hear some honest answers in

---

[9] See Tara C Dennehy and Nilanjana Dasgupta. "Female peer mentors early in college increase women's positive academic experiences and retention in engineering." *PNAS*. August 6, 2016.

return. As a mentor, actively answering questions you know the answer to but never really thought about can be eye opening.

Saying your thoughts out loud is a powerful way to lock in your own learning. And when you don't know an answer, researching together with your mentee fills a blind spot you might not have known you had. This partnership creates a strong sense of belonging and trust that will support you both.

Mentoring partnerships offer you and your mentee/mentor a safe space to explore different perspectives, challenges, and solutions. You can become more aware of your biases and even learn tools to better manage them. And don't forget, being the mentor does not preclude you from seeking your mentee's guidance.

Building Trust-Based Partnerships

The female peer mentors study published by PNAS also highlighted that open and honest mixed gender mentoring are great. Consider mentoring at least one person who doesn't remind you of you.

Use some of these questions to connect and support your new mentee's development.

- What are your personal values and goals?
- Which of your skills and abilities are most valuable to success in your career?
- Which skills do you want to develop?
- What tools will help you overcome any difficulties you experience in your role?

Actively listen to their answers.

And remember, we're all learning together. Build trust by asking your new mentee for feedback.

Find Mentees

I wager everyone has something to offer as a mentor. Let's be sure though. Take a minute to work through the following quiz.

Pop Quiz
VALUE TO POTENTIAL MENTEES

Do you have technical, leadership, and/or mom/life skills?

Select one:

YES   NO

Results

If (Yes) ⟶ Congratulations, you have skills to share with others! Someone out there can benefit from a conversation with you.

If (No) ⟶ Please review your transferable skills venn diagram (see Chapter 1). Then retake this quiz.

Based on your quiz results, you confirmed you have skills and life experience that are valuable to share with someone!

Thinking about it from a slightly different angle, what sets you apart from your peers?

Mentoring can be a purely technical partnership. One person is skilled in systems engineering, the other person needs to learn more—it's a match! Or mentoring can be purely leadership skills focused. One person has journeyed farther in their career than the other and has wisdom to share—match!

Most often it's a blend. The person you're going to mentor might not specifically want to be you when they grow up, and that's ok. Maybe you have some technical knowledge and a few communication tricks you can offer. They might have a few to offer back. Layering life experiences into these sessions can solidify the partnership and celebrate your shared experiences.

I have found my best mentoring relationships have been formed organically over time. When you find someone who shows interest in you and your growth, who you trust and respect, ask for 30 minutes on their calendar (or offer to buy them a cup of coffee). If that goes well, ask if you can make it a recurring meeting.

Similarly, if you come across a peer or earlier career person you connect with, think about making an offer to meet with them.

Awkward, yes.

Worth it? Definitely!

If you are interested in meeting technical women in a field you just don't currently have access to, consider who in your current network might. Ask them for a suggestion and an introduction. Most people are happy to help connect friends with others when it comes from a place of learning and community.

Many programs out there that pair people together. Since you are seeking lasting connections with other humans, this might feel a bit like blind dating. The upside is you will meet many interesting people you never would have connected with through your own network. The slight downside is you might want to have a friend at the ready in case you want a mid-meeting bailout call.

If you don't like the blind-date idea, here are a few slightly more organic options to consider:

- Sign up for mentoring programs through your company, affinity group, or professional organizations.
- Join the board of a non-profit organization you're excited about—this will create more opportunities for organic connections over time.
- Volunteer to peer mentor a new team member or help with new-hire onboarding.

- Practice sharing your stories by volunteering to speak about STEM at a school—not all mentoring is one on one. Answering questions with a class of excited 8-year-olds can be energizing!
- If all else fails, organize your own mentoring speed dating event where you ask each of your friends to bring at least one person the group doesn't already know. Sometimes we must create opportunities.

Now you are ready. Go find that mentee or peer mentor. Ask that leader you admire if you can meet them for a coffee.

You have so much to gain, and so much to share.

Being Us

We are here—over 3 million women and LGBTQIA+ STEM employees are working in the US today.[10] Despite a centuries old story of biases, stereotypes, family responsibilities, social norms, and ingrained cultural beliefs, 3 million of us today choose to work in STEM.

3 million is a lot of voices.

Imagine if we recorded every woman and LGBTQIA+ voice in a technical profession for even just two minutes. Each recording could be two minutes of educational accomplishments and professional choices (what they enjoy, what they don't), their hobbies and passions, and a shout out to the people they love…

At just two minutes each we would have over 11 years of voice to inspire others. Imagine that.

---

[10] According to the U.S. Bureau of Statistics, *Employment projections table 2021*, there are 9,880,200 people in STEM occupations today. Per the US census, "women are nearly half of U.S. workforce but only 27% of STEM workers." census.gov. (2021).

We can combine the 20% under-representation identified by Imperial College (see Introduction) with the Gallop report, "U.S. LGBT identification steady at 7.2%." news.gallup.com. (2023). This tells us there are approximately 415,000 LGBTQIA+ STEM professions in addition to those who also identify female.

Combining these figures, we are more than 3 million strong.

With all of us taking a role in sharing our stories we can change what the next generation sees. Maybe you want to share two minutes or maybe you can give more. What message do you want to share?

It doesn't have to be polished. It doesn't have to be deep or profound. It can be as simple as calendar notifications to let people know you are planning three vacations this year with your family. Or it could be taking a day go to the local school to simply say, "Hi, I'm an engineer."

This is your opportunity to celebrate your professional and personal successes. You can discuss where you've achieved some stability and satisfaction, and where you're still iterating.

In June 2023 I attended an international career event hosted by two fantastic non-profits, Mothers in Science and Cambridge Association for Women in Science and Engineering (CAMAWISE). The day included four keynote speakers, all of whom were moms in STEM finding their way along their journey. I heard imposter syndrome mentioned twice and many comments along the lines of "I'm not the expert, but here's what I did."

I was so happy to see the audience respond with love and support. They asked insightful questions and shared how moving they found each personal story. No one was expecting to hear the secret recipe for success. We were all looking to connect. We wanted to hear stories that reminded us we're not alone as STEM moms. It was fabulous, and I am so thankful the four keynote speakers were brave enough to share.

In STEM we are taught to solve problems. We design, build, and test until we've reached a solution. Growing women represented in technical professions is a tougher problem to solve than most, but it docsn't mean we can't make progress.

Together we can continue to share our own stories and lift other voices around us. We might never know who specifically we inspire. And I think that's ok.

Keep showing up as you, all of you, and together we're going to change how people think of STEM.

CONCLUSION

YOUR OWN BEST LIFE

I hope you are now feeling energized!

If you've been working through the activities in this hands-on adventure guide you have completed over two dozen activities. Each has focused on a part of you, your life, your career, and your quest to integrate all the above.

You have spent time considering your unique skills, values, and goals. You have artifacts in hand to guide you through major life decisions and checklists for navigating transitions.

You are empowered to choose to take opportunities that align to your big audacious goals and say no to the rest.

And on top of that, you have a set of hypothetical maps to encourage action and forward momentum. We're embracing the theory that no single map will be right, but they will all provide motivation to engage with the most intriguing versions of your life you can currently imagine. Seriously, what if that crazy map worked out!

I encourage you to spend some additional time reflecting. What you wrote down during each activity is far less important than the clarity you now feel about where you want to go and why.

If you are an ally on this journey, thank you for staying with us. Hopefully the perspectives offered have helped to deepen your own thinking. Please remember this is only one set of data points in a larger conversation—I encourage you to seek out more perspectives!

So, what now?

Reflect on a New Design

You are inspiring when you live your best life—authentic inner strength is magnetic!

What would it feel like to know you are living your very best life? Not the life you think you should have, or the life that makes most sense on paper. What is the life *you* want?

Consider the passions you want to pursue. Do you want to wholeheartedly pursue a technical career? Do you want to pursue leadership? Or parenthood? Maybe you've discovered you want something else entirely. Remind yourself that with clarity on your goals and boundaries you can do any or all of the above while maintaining a healthy and balanced lifestyle.

Dr. Karen Nyberg, the 50th woman in space, spent 180 days on the International Space Station while raising her then 3-year-old son. She also found time to develop her passion for art.[1]

Dr. Merritt Moore, professional ballerina and quantum physicist, didn't allow her passion to be blocked by previous limits on what she *should be*. By following two seemingly opposite dreams, Merritt has created a

---

[1] Watch *Like a Mother* | *Episode 3: Astronaut*. Produced by Netflix Family. (2021).

unique and exciting life dancing with her robot. She is demonstrating that anything is possible. One of her favorite mottos, "play is the highest form of research," highlights the joy one can feel when they are authentically integrating their passions into a STEM career, and a STEM mindset into their passions![2]

One more time, we'll pause and reflect. Use the space below to capture any thoughts that are coming up. Think back through all the activities and stories. What do you want to capture right now? How do you plan to leverage your powerhouse of technical, leadership, and life skills to design this life you choose to pursue?

Reflection Space: Designing Your Own Best Life

---

[2] See Laura Hiscott. "Merritt Moore: the physicist and ballet dancer mixing science and art using robots and dance." *Physicsworld*. April 11, 2023.

The intent of *STEM Moms* is not to prescribe a life or a specific path. It is an offering of tools and concepts to allow you to choose. By keeping an open mind, focusing on iterative solutions when you feel stuck, and finding opportunities to lift others along the way, you are living your best life.

Celebrate the Great Days

As a working mother of two I have tried a lot of different solutions to try to make it all work, even just for one day. Some advice I received was terrible, some was life changing. A lot of what's in this book is the fabulous morsels I then iterated on. I have two kids and a partner I love. I have led teams solving technical challenges I have thoroughly enjoyed. And a lot of the time I did it with time to spare to play volleyball or to bake a tasty treat.

But I did something wrong… I didn't celebrate it.

It seems ridiculous, but up until now I have always been highly reluctant to tell people I *only* work 40 hours a week. Reluctant is the wrong word. I was petrified.

As a leader in a Fortune 100 company, I felt like a strange alien when I first discovered I could successfully lead a highly productive team without massive unpaid overtime. Working 50 to 60 hours per week seemed to be the unwritten rule among most of my peer managers. It didn't seem to make them more productive though, and it definitely didn't make them any happier.

I would whisper my secret to mentees and small groups at round tables. "Yes, I only work 40 hours a week." They would be shocked.

But why?!

Most would agree I do excellent work. When I say I'm going to do something, I follow through. I prioritize and think systematically through complicated problems. A leader I admire once publicly thanked me for stepping into a challenging leadership role "with grace and power." There really isn't much higher praise in my book!

So why couldn't I admit I was also keeping my work to a reasonable number of hours? It almost felt like bragging, which as we all now know, we don't like to do. I knew this was a personal win. I was living my life aligned to my goals. But I wasn't celebrating it in a way that could support others with similar goals.

So, I pose this question to you… are you celebrating your wins?

It is only possible to live happily ever after on a daily basis.

Margaret Wander Bonanno

A Certain Slant of Light

If you don't feel like you're quite at the "I'm winning" stage, I encourage you to use the tools from this book to continue working toward your version of balance—and be sure to celebrate your wins along the way.

If you do feel you are making progress, don't keep it quiet like I did. Find ways to share that it can be done with people who care. Let others know you have found your version of your best life, so they can have a role model to help them find balance and happiness too.

The Geena Davis Institute on Gender in Media asserts "if she can see it, she can be it." Their STEM in the media research highlights a huge bias toward portraying STEM careers (of any gender) as incompatible with family life. A staggering 42.9% of STEM characters are shown sacrificing personal life for work.[3]

The world of media is projecting a narrative that tells us a life dedicated to STEM might be awesome, but it comes at a cost. We can make cool gadgets for James Bond and solve murders with a single soil sample, but to do so movies tell us we need to trade in self-care, family, and anything resembling a happy life.

---

[3] The Lyda Hill Foundation & The Geena Davis Institute on Gender in Media have a wealth of research and articles. Learn more at SeeJane.org.

I don't believe this narrative. I know many people who have families and technical careers they love. I am one of them, and I am not alone.

When you get to a place where you know you're thriving at work and at home, celebrate it! Write it in your success journal or capture it in your favorite app. With your newfound clarity on your goals and values, your new career marker map, and your actionable checklists in hand, you might be there now.

But then keep going. Decide who in your life could benefit from seeing you succeed and then share your truth with them.

If you're not quite there yet, remind yourself to celebrate and share a win (or micro-win) soon.

Foster Connection

I would love to keep this conversation going. The more we can share our truths the more we can connect all our separate one-woman islands. We are not alone. Let's share!

A few ideas of how we can keep sharing:

- Share a post on your social media about your truths—consider using hashtags to connect broader communities: *#Stemmoms, #STEMMomsBook, #WomeninEngineering, #mothersinscience.*
- Follow any of the above hashtags or any others you are excited about. Be sure to share likes often and leave comments to encourage ongoing conversation.
- Share your own story at mothersinscience.com/journeys—I'm so interested to hear about you and how you are navigating your adventure. Do you have other tools and tips to share?

This is only a short list. I've included a few more at the back of this book if you're interested. There are countless ways to share your story.

Enjoy finding your favorite.

Just recently I went to my son's third grade classroom to help with a math-based design project. When the teacher asked me to introduce myself, I said, "Hi, I'm Cassie. I am an engineer and I design airplanes." Short and sweet.

Instantly two little hands shot up in the air...

> *My dad is an engineer!*

> *My Grandpa was an engineer, too!*

The kids were excited I was there and wanted to connect.

I spent two hours with the class helping them translate the concept of mathematical arrays into real life applications. They chose from buildings, satellites, and city blocks. It was a wonderful project. With a little support and a couple curious questions, every single student, independent of gender, was engaged and exited to engineer.

Now maybe, just maybe, when one of the girls in that classroom grows up to be an engineer and introduces herself in her kid's class, some of the hands that shoot up might say, "my mom is an engineer, too!"

Here's hoping.

Today I'm just happy to have an opportunity to share!

Acronyms

Technical workplaces seem to love acronyms. The problem is no two companies (and sometime no two teams in the same company) use these seemingly simple letter combinations for the same purpose. Here is how I intended each of the acronyms I used in this book.

AWIS	Association for Women in Science
BEYA	Black Engineer of the Year Awards (Tagline: Becoming Everything You Are)
CAD	Computer-Aided Design
CAMAWISE	Cambridge Association for Women in Science and Engineering
ELDP	Emerging Leaders Development Program
ELM	Engineer, Leader, Mom
ELMM	Engineer, Leader, Mom, Mentor
EQ	Emotional Intelligence
HCHH	Highchair Happy Hour
LGBTQIA+	Lesbian, gay, bisexual, transgender, queer, intersex, asexual. The plus sign symbolizes the other innumerable identities included under the LGBTQ+ umbrella.[1]
MSU	Montana State University
NBER	National Bureau of Economic Research
NCES	National Center for Education Statistic
PNAS	Proceedings of the National Academy of Science of the United States of America
SMART	Specific, Measurable, Achievable, Relevant, and Time-Bound
STEM	Science, Technology, Engineering & Mathematics. Other popular variations include STEAM (A = Arts) and STEMM (second M = Medicine).
SWE	Society of Women Engineering
YOLO	You Only Live Once

---

[1] Learn more: them.us/story/what-does-lgbtq-mean-lgbtqia-stands-for-queer-history.

List of Activities

CHAPTER 4

CHAPTER 5

CONCLUSION

Find printable copies of all worksheets at:

www.elmmcoaching.com

List of Ally Notes

Acknowledgements

I am so very thankful for my amazing and ever-expanding village. I wish I could thank each and every one of you properly. Alas, I am dedicating this space to loved ones who were pivotal to the creation of this book:

To my sisters Angela and Becky, for your endless patience with my questions about em dashes and commas. I am continually inspired by how your writings convey beauty, authenticity, and humor. Thank you for your encouragement on my own writing journey.

To my dad, for always treating me like the engineer you knew I would become. Thank you for using my "some-assembly-required" toys as an opportunity to teach me what a Phillips head is and for every moment you spent pondering calculus homework with me.

To my mom, for creatively iterating on what motherhood could be with an incredible abundance of love and patience. She created magic.

To Pat, for being my partner, best friend, and the love of my life. I am so thankful we've chosen to share this dynamic and unpredictable adventure together.

And to our boys… you are a joy to know and raise. I am so proud of how kind and fun you both are. Thank you for not being too cool to hang with your parents… yet.

To Ann Stevens, for inviting Christina Willis, Tracey Espero, Rochelle Friedman, and myself to join you on stage at WE21. The experience of sharing our journeys out loud was *STEM Moms'* first spark.

And to Jake Turner & Ryan Cantor, for helping shape *STEM Moms* from the very beginning. Your excitement and curiosity to engage when this book was nothing more than a stack of yellow sticky notes was the encouragement I needed to keep moving forward. Thank you.

About the Publisher

ELMM Press is a publishing company dedicated to increasing diversity in STEM. We publish books and resources that reflect the experiences and perspectives of underrepresented groups, including women, mothers, LGBTQIA+ people, and people of color.

We believe that everyone has the potential to succeed in STEM, regardless of their background. That's why we're committed to making STEM more inclusive and accessible to everyone.

We do this by:

- Publishing books and resources that feature characters from underrepresented groups.
- Providing mentorship and support to aspiring authors.
- Partnering with organizations dedicated to raising awareness of the importance of diversity in STEM.

We know that representation matters. When young people see themselves reflected in the books they read, they are more likely to believe that they can achieve their dreams. That's why we're committed to creating a platform for diverse voices to shine.

Visit www.elmm.press to get involved in our mission.

About the Author

Cassie Leonard is a mom on a mission!

Motivated by her passion to grow the face of women and mothers in STEM, she is sharing the tools that have aided her on her own quest for a balanced and fulfilling life as an engineer, leader, mom, and mentor.

In her 16 years in the aerospace industry, Cassie grew from an entry level structural analyst to the senior mechanical engineering leader in a half billion-dollar division. She was recognized in 2020 and 2021 for "significant contributions to the company's success," the same two years her children were suddenly at home full time.

In 2022, Cassie left corporate life to focus her efforts on supporting Engineers, Leaders, and Moms. She is now the proud founder, CEO, and principal coach at ELMM Coaching. As a certified executive and leadership development coach, she is excited to work with anyone seeking to live their best life!

In support of her passion for elevating the voices of STEM moms, Cassie is also an executive team member at Mothers in Science, a nonprofit investing in research, advocacy, and sharing journeys!

Cassie and her husband Patrick live in the beautiful Pacific Northwest with their two wonderful sons. She is walking the tightrope of full-time leader, full time mom, and full-time person. Most days it goes well, some days it does not.

To stay active and mentally sane, Cassie plays beach volleyball all spring and summer, races cyclocross in the fall, and cross-country skis in the winter.

Connect with Cassie!

Email	cassie@ELMMcoaching.com
Instagram	@cassie_finding_balance

Will You Share the Love?

Get *STEM Moms* for a friend, associate, mentee, or family member!

If you have found *STEM Moms* valuable and know others who would too, consider buying them a copy as a gift. While written from the lens of a mom in engineering, the tools and tricks within have the potential to be valuable to so many people in your circle.

Special bulk discounts are available if you would like your whole team or organization to benefit from reading this.

Just contact cassie@elmmcoaching.com
or visit www.elmmcoaching.com.

Would You Like Cassie Leonard to Speak to Your Organization?

Book Cassie Now!

Cassie accepts a limited number of speaking and workshop engagements each year. Content and durations can be customized to meet your team's needs.

To learn how you can bring her message into your business, non-profit, school, or HCHH, email cassie@elmmcoaching.com or visit www.elmmcoaching.com.

More Ways to Grow Diversity in STEM

If you are excited for more, here's a bonus checklist for you!

Bonus Checklist
SUPPORTING &
CONNECTING

☐ **Join the LinkedIn Group: STEM Moms.**

This community continues the conversation with likeminded proponents of women and mothers in STEM.

☐ **Post a review.**

Encourage others to get involved by leaving a review for this book wherever you bought your copy.

☐ **Be an ally.**

Advocate for women, LGBTQIA+ people, and all other underrepresented groups in STEM.

☐ **Get personalized support from the author.**

Author Cassie Leonard, a certified executive coach, is offering personalized support to help you apply the lessons from her book to your own life. Book your FREE 30-minute Discovery Call at elmmcoaching.com today!

Use this as a starting point, then get creative.
Best wishes as you find and support your own herd of unicorns!

Printed in Great Britain
by Amazon

53719600R00090